PRAISE FOR *BETTER TO CRY NOW*

"Geoffrey Newman's brave book is awe inspiring. He takes us on a treacherous journey of self-discovery, where he invites us into vivid scenes of joy, pain, sorrow, anger, love, disappointment, triumph, and redemption as he searches for identity. Geoffrey was profoundly instrumental in my own development as a young drama student at Howard University. And now he is taking that seasoned wisdom to others in the form of this book. I am certain that *Better To Cry Now* will not only change but indeed save people's lives. In this harsh and cruel time that we live in, what a gift it is to receive such a precious flower."

—RALPH REMINGTON, Director of Cultural Affairs, San Francisco Arts Commission

"*Better to Cry Now* holds significant meaning and value from my perspective, for it chronicles a pathway to one's very best life in the presence of existential obstacles. Geoffrey's journey narrates the life of a charming, optimistic, gay, Black man who had the creativity and tenacity to live life on his terms. Geoffrey's vision for his dazzling future was the catalyst that catapulted him toward living his *brightest story* in every area of his professional and personal life."

—SANDRA BOWIE, award-winning actress; vice-chair, National Guild for Community Arts Education; former vice president for arts education, New Jersey Performing Arts Center; former executive director, Billie Holiday Theater, New York

"Geoffrey Newman has written a memoir that is engaging, honest, hopeful, and purposeful. He reminds us that the emotional scars and wounds we carry within us begin to heal when first we confront the pains that caused them with perception and honesty, and then when we take positive action, committing ourselves to the process of change in how we see ourselves, how we see others (not as adversaries or challenges, but as flawed human beings like ourselves), and in how we see our world around us (not as a space that exists only as a force that acts upon us, but as a space in which we can experience our best selves). It is then that we can construct a space in which we can be, finally, unafraid."

—RICHARD E. WESLEY, associate professor, NYU Tisch School of the Arts

"Newman's career memoir illustrates strategies to forge ahead by staying focused on one's vision for success and staying true to the person we are. His story provides the reader with a role model that chronicles the multiple challenges one may confront as a Black child, fine arts student, performer, faculty member, musical theatre director, department head, and Black gay man. I enthusiastically recommend Newman's *Better to Cry Now*."

—MAURICE J. SEVIGNY, PHD, Dean Emeritus, College of Fine Arts, University of Arizona

"Reading *Better to Cry Now* is like having a conversation with a wise old friend. His life is a classic American success story, with the Civil Rights and Gay Rights movements as part of the backdrop of his life. He has both lived through changing times and helped to change the times. I admire his perseverance and unflagging good cheer. In a time when reactionary forces are trying to devalue concepts like diversity and inclusion, his life is a vivid reminder of the importance of both."

—CHIP DEFFAA, award-winning author and playwright and former music and theater critic for the *New York Post*

"The adventures of one who finds his way from the hidden worlds of Blacks passing as whites and gays passing as heterosexuals are told in a manner that reveals lessons learned at each encounter. Holistically and introspectively, educator and performer/director Geoffrey Newman invites the reader on a journey, not just about how he was shaped by personal experiences and how he shaped others, but also how he gained an ever deeper understanding and empathy for the life of the everyman."

—RONALD L. SHARPS, Associate Dean, College of the Arts, Montclair State University

BETTER TO CRY NOW

SHAPING THE FLOW OF A GAY BLACK MAN

GEOFFREY NEWMAN

RIVER GROVE
BOOKS

This book is a memoir reflecting the author's present recollections of experiences over time. Its story and its words are the author's alone. Some details and characteristics may be changed, some events may be compressed, and some dialogue may be recreated.

Published by River Grove Books
Austin, TX
www.rivergrovebooks.com

Copyright © 2024 Geoffrey Wayne Newman

All rights reserved.

Thank you for purchasing an authorized edition of this book and for complying with copyright law. No part of this book may be reproduced, stored in a retrieval system, or transmitted by any means, electronic, mechanical, photocopying, recording, or otherwise, without written permission from the copyright holder.

Distributed by River Grove Books

Design and composition by Greenleaf Book Group and Mimi Bark
Cover design by Greenleaf Book Group and Mimi Bark
Cover art: This expressionistic portrait of Geoffrey Newman was painted by David Driskell in 1967 and then gifted by Mr. Driskell to the author.

Publisher's Cataloging-in-Publication data is available.

Print ISBN: 978-1-63299-867-5

eBook ISBN: 978-1-63299-868-2

First Edition

*This book is dedicated to my parents,
Arthur Eugene Newman and Bertha Battle Newman,
whose support throughout my life provided
the shoulders on which I stand today.*

All the world's a stage,
and all the men and women merely players:
they have their exits and their entrances;
and one man in his time plays many parts . . .
—WILLIAM SHAKESPEARE

CONTENTS

PROLOGUE

xi

ACT 1:

Striving (1956–1964)   1

ACT 2:

Hiding (1963–1974)   33

ACT 3:

Emerging (1975–1987)   109

ACT 4:

Belonging (1988–2014)   175

EPILOGUE (2023)

239

PROLOGUE

My lifelong goal has been, and continues to be, finding the confidence to believe in myself. I have always been concerned about fitting in and being accepted, willingly meeting the expectations others might have of me and how they see me. I believed for years that I should try to be what others wanted me to be: play, as best as I could, the various roles others defined for me, trying desperately to fit in with the people around me. Thus, my goal has often been figuring out what I should do to achieve the acceptance of others. When I thought I was on the right track, I often validated and measured my success by what others would say. At first, it was what my parents said. Then, it was what my teachers said. Later, in public schools, I used my performance on standardized tests and the grades I achieved in my courses as my measure of success. When I entered the workplace, I relied on what my colleagues said about me and how my supervisors rated my work performance. You see, I never felt completely comfortable evaluating my success. You will also see as my story unfolds that I had to learn to face life's challenges guided by my sense of self, not what others wanted me to be. I had to learn to trust my intuition and gain pride from within.

It was, however, through education that I learned how to grow and be happy with who I am. It was also through education that I learned how to accept and unconditionally love others and myself. It was education that provided me with the courage to flourish in the most difficult of environments, unclear pathways, and confusing times. I had to learn how to make sense of where chaos appeared to reign, where conflict produced negative messages, and where self-doubt was imminent.

You see, like most people, my journey was never easy. Enormous obstacles appeared in my way of achieving lofty personal and professional goals. It often seemed that just as I vaulted over one hurdle, another and then another one even more difficult than the previous one muscled into my path. I had great parents who nurtured and loved me. They always provided me with helpful, loving guidance and strong, reassuring direction. Yet I still had to discover who I was and wanted to become, then find the courage to pursue my unique path, however unreachable it seemed. This book shares that journey.

ACT 1

STRIVING (1956-1964)

My French teacher at Calvin Coolidge Public High School in Washington, DC, made a troubling announcement on my first day of tenth grade.

"Neither Black people nor Jews have the capability to master the French language," he said. "So if you fall into either category, you must drop my class, as you are going to fail."

Someone asked him about the French-speaking countries in Africa and the West Indies where locals speak French as their native language. He did not hesitate.

"What they speak is a poor version of French," he replied. "You can say that those countries speak a bastardized version of French, not the language as it should be spoken. I teach French as it is spoken in France."

The year was 1962, quite a volatile one. All around America, frustration and negativity reigned. Every day, you heard of some tragedy. The country was changing. People in authority felt it was time to assert control, reinforce rules, and keep people in line. This idea was particularly true for tenured public-school teachers, entrenched in their roles for many years. So, shocking as my teacher's words were, they came as no surprise.

My parents took what he said as a challenge. First, we went to the school principal. I listened as my mother, a teacher herself, made a case that I should be taken out of the class. She demanded to know how such a racist, bigoted teacher could be allowed to remain in any classroom at a public school. To our surprise, the principal was meek, a very timid man not wanting to engage in any dialogue concerning one of his tenured teachers.

"That's not my decision," he told my parents. "He has strong connections in the Office of the Superintendent of Schools. There's nothing I can do."

My mother rarely took no for an answer. No one intimidated her, particularly if one of her children was in jeopardy. The next thing I knew, I was in the waiting room of the superintendent's office as my parents prepared for an audience with this high-level administrator. When he appeared at the entrance of his office and saw my parents, he seemed surprised. The superintendent looked to me like a powerful, self-important, huge white man who had no experience dealing with two highly educated, articulate, and well-informed Black parents. But these Black parents were on a mission. I was told to remain in the outer office while my parents entered this autocrat's inner sanctum. I vigilantly listened while acting as if I could not hear what they were saying. But it was not difficult to hear what was happening.

While both my parents were present, my mother, a certified teacher in this public-school system, took the lead in making the case for their son. I easily made out my parents' loud yet respectful voices as they took control of the situation. The meeting seemed to go on forever as I patiently waited for it to end. Clearly, my parents had no intention of leaving the superintendent's office without achieving a satisfactory outcome.

Shortly after our visit, I was moved into the other overcrowded French class, led by a different teacher who, at least, did not harbor the same negative feelings as the previous one. My parents' efforts paid off, but my struggles in learning continued. *What a way to start learning another language*, I thought. Coolidge only offered the two French classes on the College Preparatory Track. My new class was oversubscribed and well beyond the limit of twenty-five students. Students were expected to learn what they didn't accomplish in what they called "language laboratories." These were very sanitized small spaces that contained headphones, with partitions separating the students. They looked like little prison environments stripped of everything, lacking warmth, pictures, or representations of countries and people outside the United States. This was not a space that seemed designed to make me feel welcomed or motivated to learn a new language. Once again, I felt discouraged. Placement in this class was better, but the new French teacher struggled to give students the individualized attention they needed. We students seemed to be mostly on our own in or out of the language lab.

Even worse, if a student did not satisfactorily complete this beginning-level French class, they had little hope of completing the two-year Romance language requirement of the College Preparatory Track or getting accepted into a college. I could have studied German—the other prep language open to students in this track—but those classes were also oversubscribed to students. Spanish was not considered a fulfillment of the language requirement for college and was not even offered to college prep students—another glaring example of the pernicious prejudices operating in the larger society.

Once again, it appeared I was stuck in a situation where I would have to make it work, whether I liked it or not.

In addition to my French class debacle, during a teacher–parent conference, my homeroom teacher told my parents, as I sat and listened, that I did not have college potential.

"Even if Geoffrey is lucky enough to get a college to admit him," she said, "he will most certainly drop out or fail."

That conference was the culmination of many lessons I had learned over the years. I was a Black student in a white system. The first lesson came in fourth grade, when I had to pack up and walk to the all-white school in Southeast Washington, DC, so my light-skinned Black face could add color to the pale student body. No one there looked or sounded like me. At eight, I thought that was the worst thing that could happen to me. I seemed far behind the white students. The teachers rarely called on me. When I raised my hand to answer a question, I was always surprisingly wrong or embarrassed. I felt like I had been poorly prepared or missed something. My self-esteem went down the tubes. I constantly wondered if what I had been previously taught provided any value at all in this new environment.

Slowly, I realized my education was in my own hands. I could only succeed if I took control of my learning process. I needed help. That's when my mother, who understood the discriminatory practices of the public schools, made her signature move. From fourth grade until I started high school, she insisted that I come home every day after school and review my daily lesson by sharing what had happened in the classroom with her. She would then help me prepare for the next day of class. I cried and yelled. I didn't like this plan.

"It's not fair!" I said. "Everyone else gets to go out and play, and I have to study with you."

Every time, she had the same reply. "Better to cry now than be sorry later," she said. She waited as I dried my tears. I would always trust her words, finish my work, and prepare for the next day in class. My mother was seldom wrong in advice or direction. And she possessed the patience of Job.

One day, in sixth grade, my mother determined I had a bad cold or something worse.

"You're staying home from school," she said. "You need a day in bed to recover." The choice was serious for her. As I lay in bed, wondering if I could slip downstairs and watch television, I heard a knock on my door. When I opened it, I saw a student from my class. He told me the teacher had sent him to say to me that IQ testing would start that afternoon, that I must return to school, and that if I didn't, I would not continue into junior high school. This new "track testing" was for placement in the Basic, General, College Preparatory, or Honors tracks.

"Okay, I'll get dressed and meet you back at school," I said, thinking my classmate's message must be important if the teacher sent a student to my home. I got dressed and went to school. As my cold worsened, I could only hope I would make it through the barrage of testing that faced me.

When I returned home that day and my mother arrived home from work, I explained what had transpired. She hit the roof. She said I had no business getting out of bed and going to school without her permission, regardless of what the teacher had said. I'd thought I didn't have a choice, that I *had to* get out of bed and sit for these standardized tests, regardless of how I felt. I had been told there would be no makeup examinations, regardless of the circumstances. But my mother told me I was just wrong. She explained that a student's health greatly affects how well or poorly they perform on tests, particularly standardized examinations.

That day, I learned I should always listen to my parents—not just my teachers—for direction and guidance. Education at home became as crucial as it was in the classroom. According to my parents, Black children could not be content with just being equal; we had to be better. They also said that not all teachers were equally eager to help Black children succeed. I understood and accepted that I needed to work hard and then even harder. Nothing else mattered. I had to meet and surpass people's demands, including teachers, who did not necessarily like me sharing their time, space, or resources. I would just have to learn to overcome those hostile forces and the many difficulties and obstacles put in my path.

Also, I rarely performed up to my potential on standardized testing, which seemed to be the primary public-school tool for assessing and evaluating the progress and potential of all students. Not until much later in life did I discover I had test anxiety. I'd often get tense just walking into the room for a test. Plus, there were time limits. Everyone was expected to finish within the same allotted time. That requirement always sent me into a panic. I was well into college before realizing I was creating this problem by not setting my own pace through an examination. The more I learned to relax regardless of imposed time constraints, the easier it became to take tests.

However, teachers, particularly white teachers, appeared to focus on how only the Black students failed to perform under pressure, implying a weakness in our intellects. Additionally, white teachers seemed to have arrived at an unspoken conclusion that Black students were better suited for the Basic or General tracks, that they were not College Preparatory material and certainly not Honors material. The teachers often encouraged the Black children to learn a good trade.

My parents felt that education was the answer to a good life, a satisfying career, and personal happiness. They repeatedly stressed the importance of education to my brother and me, and they acted on that assumption not only for their children but for themselves. My mother had finished college (then called Emmanuel Missionary College, later changed to Andrews University), and my father, at that time, was finishing his degree at night at The American University.

In that era, public schools were not yet air-conditioned, making the end of the school year particularly brutal. During May and June in Washington, DC, the high humidity, combined with overcrowded conditions, made it difficult, at times impossible, to focus on daily studies. I had to repeatedly tell myself that education was not meant to be easy but would pay off in the end. I persevered.

But nothing came easy. My entire public-school education was a struggle. White teachers resented being forced to teach Black children because of public-school integration. In 1954, the US Supreme Court ruled unanimously in *Brown v. Board of Education* that racial segregation in public schools was unconstitutional; this landmark decision called for the immediate integration of all public schools in the United States. In Washington, DC, the decision forced white schools to enroll Black students in the middle of the academic year.

Despite the many people who disagreed with implementing this decision, I was informed during Christmas vacation that after the holidays, I would start a new school with new teachers and students in a new building much farther from where I currently attended. I remember when that day came. The walk to school was different, not just because of the new route but also because of the growing fear of what this new school had in store for me.

I recall approaching a building so unique that it was unlike anything I had ever seen. The children clustered around the entrance of the building were standing outside in the cold, and whether or not true, in my mind, they all seemed to be looking at me, wondering whether I had lost my way and was in the wrong place at the wrong time. Boy, was this scary. I swallowed hard and kept moving forward, going directly to the principal's office, where I was to check in. In the main office, no one seemed particularly friendly, welcoming, or even warm. My check-in was handled like a vending machine: fill this out, here are your books, and this is where you are to go.

"Now be on your way," I remember being told. That seemed like one of the longest and scariest days of my life. I can only recall that it finally ended, and I ran home to report that I had survived to live another day.

This is me at (I think) the age of three or four in an outfit my mother made for me. She made all my clothes for the first six years of my life.

So I often found myself in a place where I was never welcomed and not at all wanted. Consequently, I frequently struggled with a lack of confidence. I regularly heard from my teachers what I was doing wrong and seldom heard words of encouragement, achievement, or anything I could do to make it better. An additional complication existed: I was in the large baby boomer generation, so every classroom was physically too small for the number of students crammed into the space. Planning for this large generation of students was never reflected in the physical structures built to accommodate instruction. I would often come into a room and find a seat or go to another empty classroom and bring in an extra chair if I wanted to sit.

However, after overcoming the French class debacle, adjusting to small spaces, and dealing with inadequate classroom ventilation and dismissive teachers, I developed a life outside the classroom, and things got a bit brighter. I found a love for music and a passion for making it.

After enrolling in Davis Elementary School, I wanted to play a musical instrument, which was not an option in the all-Black school. I wanted to learn piano. However, the new school told me no piano instruction was available since I'd transferred in the middle of the school year. The only available music instruction was for the violin. *Violin?* I thought. *Who studies violin?* I decided to give it a try. As it turned out, playing violin taught me how to read music on the treble clef. When I got to junior high school, I switched to trombone, which taught me to read music on the bass clef. Combining the two, I learned to read all sheet music and learned how to sight-read music.

I also discovered I had a propensity for playing trombone and making music, which opened an opportunity for me to join the John Philip Sousa Junior High School marching band program. And, just like that, I found a new family of support: the kids in the marching band and the teachers who directed us. My reluctance to face school each day quickly changed. I eagerly anticipated band practice after school. The discipline I learned in the band gave me a sense of pride because I was part of something much bigger than myself. On the front line of the marching band, I enjoyed the cheers of the crowds during halftime, when we performed on the football field. After the football season ended, we became a concert band.

This school, John Philip Sousa Junior High School, was named after the great marching band composer.[1] Its band program was touted as one of the best in the country. I remember a cold and snowy day when we were chosen to play in the inaugural parade for President Dwight David Eisenhower. It was so cold that I thought my mouth would permanently stick to the mouthpiece of my trombone. But it did not. I knew I was on the front line, and we were the first group of players the world would see marching down Pennsylvania Avenue, so the cold, the blistering winds, and my feet that felt almost frozen with each step did not matter. We were on national television for the world to see, and I was on the front line of the band. Besides, my excitement, adrenaline, and determination provided me with more than enough spit and sweat to compensate for the frigid weather. I loved the applause and enjoyed the intensity of the music-making process as the band marched down that street in step with precision. Each time a note emerged from my mouth, I was thrilled. My love for music made everything else worthwhile. It made whatever troubles I felt melt away like warm butter in the hot sun. I grew more and more self-confident as I found a path that worked for me. This was the beginning—the path I knew I could pursue with success.

I had not only my own experiences of life and prejudice to draw from. I was acutely aware of my family legacies, which my parents generously shared and explained.

---

1   My parents saved up money to purchase a semidetached home in Northwest Washington, DC, a previously white-only housing district, and enrolled my brother and me in one of the top public junior and senior high schools in the city.

Striving (1956–1964)

My father descended from one of the most infamously labeled groups of people in Washington, DC—the "We-Sorts," an unfortunate government term that some considered offensive. It identified the Newman, Proctor, Swann, and Wright families, many of whom were light-skinned. According to family lore, they immigrated to the United States to free themselves from indentured servitude in England. Upon arrival in the United States, they often chose to pass for white and remained self-isolated from the general Black population. Later, they were called separationists.

My great-grandparents on the Newman side of the family.
I'm told they were the first generation of We-Sorts in the Newman family.

The We-Sorts intermarried with brothers, sisters, or first cousins to keep the family roots pure or as close to white as possible.

Eventually, the State of Maryland passed laws prohibiting siblings from marrying each other based on the practices of these families.[2] Newman relatives told me that some of our family members even married Native Americans in an effort to self-identify as non-Black people.

Black people often resented the ability of light-skinned Blacks to hide their Negro background and move more easily within a segregated society. Yet white people would feel deceived and harbored feelings of anger if a light-skinned Black person was exposed as having Black blood. In this country, mixed-race people have always had trouble being accepted or included in either racial group. So they often hid their true ethnicity except within their own family, among themselves. Mine was no exception.

Many times, when traveling with my parents, I listened to strangers try to label or ask my mother or father whether they were Hispanic, Latin, Puerto Rican, or Native American. My parents just smiled and never directly answered the comments or questions. They would say, "What do you think?"

Being light-skinned, I had to reckon with and reconcile all these factors while growing up. Adages abounded: "The lighter your skin, the brighter your opportunities." "The straighter your hair, the more you fit the American ideal." "White was right, and Black had to step back." These realities were constantly in my thoughts. I always worried. *I am not white enough, and my hair is not straight enough.*

---

[2] Justia. "2010 Maryland Code Family Law Title 2: Marriage, Subtitle 2: Valid Marriages; Void Marriages," accessed April 25, 2024, https://law.justia.com/codes/maryland/2010/family-law/title-2/subtitle-2/2-202.

Striving (1956–1964)

Before the Civil War, my mother's ancestors were enslaved on a Louisiana plantation. They were often forced into nonconsensual sexual relationships with the plantation master and became the victims of sexual exploitation. When light-skinned babies resulted from these unions, those children were raised in the main house, removed from working in the sugarcane and cotton fields, and called "house Negroes." When enslaved Black people were finally freed, my mother's family migrated to Ohio to find work and an opportunity for a better life.

My parents, Arthur and Bertha Newman, in 1985, when they were in their early sixties. I love remembering their supportive smiles and well-groomed look.

Her mother was a Battle who married a Battle. Growing up, they even lived on the same street but were not related at all. Back then, when slaves were freed, they took the names of their enslavers. Prior to that time, they were identified only by number and first name. In fact, my mother's ancestors, who were formerly enslaved people, claimed ownership of the plantation on which they were forced to live and work.

Like my father, my mother came from a large family with modest financial resources. They all possessed a profound respect and passion for education as the means for bettering themselves. Envisioning brighter futures for themselves and their children, they developed strategies for making their dreams a reality, often overcoming overwhelming odds in the process. My parents would not compromise when it came to education, even if that meant they had to work even harder and longer hours to provide better opportunities for my brother and me.

No doubt, their resolve was modeled by my grandparents on my mother's side. Blacks were not allowed to own property within the city limits of Elyria, Ohio, in the 1890s, so my mother's parents purchased seven acres just outside the city limits. Because their acreage wasn't part of the city, they could develop it as farmland. Years later, their plot became part of the city limits and was eventually sold. In the final analysis, that land proved to be a wise and most profitable investment.

My grandparents on my mother's side, Georgia and Morris Battle.
They rarely took any pictures. This is one of the few surviving photos we have of them.

The farmland designation benefited my grandparents in another way. They developed several acres for growing grapes that supplied

Welch's, the famed grape juice company. Their farm was the only vineyard when population growth expanded the city limits.

My mother, the youngest of her siblings, was the first in her family to go to college and expected the same for her two children. Her admonishment—"Better to cry now than be sorry later"—rang through my early years. Throughout my life, it helped me embrace the tough work of learning and growing.

Besides being our academic driving force, my mother was our family oral historian. She conveyed to my brother and me the rich stories and traditions of her family and my father's. What an expert, entertaining storyteller she was. Seventh-day Adventists could only engage in nonsecular activities during the Sabbath (sunset Friday to sunset Saturday). So every Saturday afternoon after church, my mother would sit with my brother and me and share many uplifting stories from our family lore. She told us how our great-grandfather walked more than 500 miles to start his own farm, where he was free of discrimination, and how he was the first in the city to own a Model T Ford. When our grandfather became a Seventh-day Adventist, she told us, he freed all his swine, which ran throughout the town, causing the neighbors to believe he must have lost his mind.

From my ancestors' struggles, my mother taught my brother and me to embrace obstacles as tools from which we could grow stronger and wiser. We learned great life lessons about survival, perseverance, the importance of making financial investments, and ownership.

I also learned that in order to love and respect others, I first had to love and respect myself. Sometimes, that lesson took enormous courage because I had to confront tremendous self-doubt and my fear of the unknown. I learned to question taking the easy path or making the most convenient decision. I learned, too, that it was possible to achieve immeasurable joys and long-lasting happiness and that tenacity in the face of life's struggles had its benefits. So, too, did drive, focus, self-motivation, self-confidence, and a deep, never-ending understanding of the value of personal growth. I discovered, or perhaps inherited, endurance, fortitude, courage, and strength of character.

My brother and I enjoyed the carefully spun turns and thrills of these exciting stories, their unexpected consequences, and their unexpected outcomes. In my mother's stories, I developed my thirst for adventure and a love for exploring uncharted pathways. They fed my endlessly inquisitive nature for discovering the world's many mysteries and what they had to offer. In short, I learned to dream, and one of my greatest dreams was to be as inspirational a teacher as she was.

My brother, Artie, and me, just before I entered first grade in 1951, in matching outfits made by my mother. Take a look at that lovely bruise on my forehead—I was always running into something!

My parents' pride in me was palpable: they consistently showered me with praise and approbation all my life. Their pleasure in my achievements was, perhaps, accentuated by my brother's troubled path. Although he consistently tested high on those standardized tests that so bedeviled me and possessed enormous potential, Artie never did well at college. My parents sent him to three schools,

Striving (1956–1964)

including Howard. Eventually, each institution told him and my parents that he should pursue other options.

Artie's inability to succeed in higher education was always a shock for me. I thought of Artie as much smarter than I was. Clearly, potential and ability were not enough for success; you needed the courage to face what life threw at you and find a path through it. Artie fought the battles I chose to outmaneuver. Perhaps he was braver. Perhaps I was craftier. In any event, he accrued bruises while I garnered applause.

Artie was nineteen months older and very much enjoyed his position as "the junior," the next in line after our father. He seldom missed an opportunity to show me I was number two and tell me I should be grateful for that position. A football tackle from a very young age, he was always bigger. I was thin and two inches shorter. That may not sound like much, but he felt that fact entitled him to be the third parent when our parents were not present or paying attention to us. If he liked a food at the dinner table, he would eat it rapidly and then coax me into giving him my portion or just take it.

My mother shared the story of how we were all out at a picnic one afternoon. I was a toddler, and Artie was not much older. It was a glorious sunny day. My father was lying on the blanket with my mother and me when Artie asked him to play ball. Having worked hard all week, my father just wanted a quick nap.

Not wanting no as an answer, Artie picked up a Coke bottle from the food basket and struck my father in the head with it.

"This is *my* time to play!" he said, pouting. "I want you to play!"

Artie never cried or said he was sorry. Fortunately, my father was not badly hurt and took Artie's demands as a child wanting to be loved by his father. So he got to his feet and played catch with Artie as my mother and I looked on.

That day, we all learned that Artie felt he should always be the center of attention and that he'd do just about anything to get it. Unfortunately, Artie believed that if he demanded hard enough or forced his way, he could be successful—not necessarily the lesson my parents wanted to teach. The incident marked the start of a repeated behavior that Artie came to regret in later years.

Another day, when Artie and I were alone, he sought me out where I was playing.

"I have a secret that you should know," he told me. "If you promise to give me your macaroni and cheese at dinner tonight, I will tell you." Mac and cheese was one of his favorite dishes.

"Okay," I replied. "Tell me."

"Mom and Dad haven't told you, but you were adopted. You were left on the doorstep one night. They took you in and eventually decided, after much thinking about it, to adopt you. You looked so pitiful."

Crushed, I broke into tears. As soon as my parents returned, I asked them, against Artie's wishes, whether what he said was true.

"Don't listen to Artie," my mother said. "He's just jealous of you."

"We love you both equally," my father added.

From then on, whenever one of us had a birthday, we both got presents. When Christmas came around, we were both equally showered with gifts. And, yes, Artie was the one who told me there was no Santa Claus.

"The presents are from Mom and Dad," he said. "You should just grow up."

I never followed my brother's path. In fact, since we grew up so close in age, I would often wait until he had bullied his way through a particular challenge, and then, as he frequently failed, my plan was to do the exact opposite. Because we approached problem-solving differently, a painful separation between my brother and me continued throughout our adult life.

Whenever we were together as adults, we argued bitterly or disagreed about everything. If I said the sky was blue, he would argue for a different color. He was very much the bully all his life until the end. He liked to control everything and everyone around him, including my parents, in their senior years. He believed controlling others was the way to get what he wanted in the world, and getting what he wanted was always his goal.

I saw how this obsession, this need for control, could ruin one's life by creating more obstacles than clear pathways. He had an opinion about every subject. He thought he could do any task he encountered better than anyone else. Lack of confidence was never a shortcoming. If he had problems achieving a goal, in his eyes, the obstacles were created by others, never by him. He never failed in his eyes but was only hampered or blocked by others. It was always someone else's fault for his lack of success.

My brother, Artie, at Christmas in 1993, in the oversized chair he replicated in his own house—his throne.

He liked people who could do something for him. He saw his life as transactional, always. What was in it for him? This was his professional face, as well as the face he showed his family and friends. On the outside, he always appeared harsh—the big, rugged football linebacker who could not be tackled, trying never to show that he really cared for anything or anyone. He was just a brute force who could hold the front line. But I came to believe that on the inside, he was a frightened little boy crying out for help and love, never understanding why he was so misunderstood and never shown enough love, the love he deserved. He fell into a trap: he enjoyed ordering people around and instructing them about what they should do even though he was often unsuccessful in his life. He seldom, if ever, learned from his mistakes. From his perspective, he already knew everything. And if he didn't know it already, it wasn't worth knowing.

Nothing was ever too much. He could handle as much as he wanted. When he married and built his own home, he purchased a massive oversized chair that became his throne. He sat on this huge piece of furniture and ordered his wife to get him a beer or water as if she were his valet, his servant. He tried to dominate everyone and, more often than not, succeeded. Those successes only led him to feel he could control even more.

Because he weighed at least 300 pounds, he eventually developed severe diabetes. Toward the end of his life, when he experienced kidney failure, his temperament mellowed. He became milder, less critical of others, less demanding. I assumed this disease caused the change in him. It was something he could not control. Yet he had caused it by his overeating, drinking, and his incessant belief in excess. He had no choice but to realize that his actions had great consequences and that there was always a price to pay. Disease has a way of teaching lessons we may not ever want to learn but learn nonetheless.

Eventually, Artie had total kidney failure and needed a transplant. Unfortunately, before that was even possible, he would have to lose at least a hundred pounds, which took much more discipline than he possessed. Artie accepted his condition and mortality and developed a newfound concern for others. During the last three years of his life, he spent three to four days out of seven at the dialysis center, where he became known as the patient who uplifted others' spirits and motivated them when they became discouraged. The doctors noted his positive attitude, charming ways, and words of encouragement. They said he lived much longer than usual for patients with total kidney failure on dialysis.

In my mind, he became a much sweeter, nicer, and caring human before he died peacefully in his sleep one night. In the end, he allowed that humble, loving little boy inside to finally emerge as the man he wanted to be.

After my brother died in 2008 at age sixty-three, I felt blessed that I had been given the opportunity to know Artie and to have had the chance to love him. He was an important teacher and guide in my life without us ever truly realizing it. When faced with the threat of being drafted into the Vietnam War after graduating from Howard, I drew on the example of my brother's bravado and refused to give in to fear. I continued to make decisions for my future with confidence, fortitude, and aggressiveness, not allowing my fears to control my life. That was all thanks to my big brother, Arthur Eugene Newman Jr.

My life started to change, and I found my path because of one magical choice: I went outside my comfort zone and pursued a part in *Guys and Dolls*, the high school musical. I could really sing, or so my high school drama and music teachers told me. Much to my parents' surprise and despite my nerves, I tried out for a part. The audition was held on the auditorium stage, where the production would be performed. As I walked in and sat in the audience, I saw that many of the students assembled for the audition also looked uneasy. Somehow, that observation made me feel more relaxed. It appeared I wasn't alone.

In a way, this is like the marching band, I thought. *All I have to do is listen and trust that I can deliver whatever they ask of me.* I had been in the church choir conducted by my godmother and found that when I followed her direction, things worked out for the best. I tried to distract myself from the fear and focus on the outcome.

"Geoffrey Newman!" someone called out. They read from the list I had signed on the wall in the hallway that morning. Hesitantly, I stood. They asked me to come to the stage. I walked slowly. *What the heck am I about to get into?* The teachers read my nervousness and spoke comforting words.

"It's all right," one said. "We just want to hear you sing. What can you sing for us?"

I have no memory of what I sang. Next, they asked me to listen to a pianist perform a vocal line from the show and then sing it. I had a good ear and could easily pick up vocal passages. The more they asked me to do, the easier performing seemed. My comfort level grew stronger. I enjoyed being onstage. It felt like singing at home. Our house was always filled with music. My father, who was in the church choir, loved to go around the house singing one tune or another. My mother loved to listen to Johnny Mathis.

Then they asked me to perform a simple dance step—cross my

leg and step back in rhythm. Though unfamiliar, the move came naturally. I left that audition thinking, *That was a lot of fun. It would be a kick to maybe get a small part.*

To my surprise, I got the lead, cast as Sky Masterson, and a period of excelling began. I found my love for performance and entertainment. They opened up my world and gave me more self-confidence than I could have ever imagined. Before the theater, only my parents had told me I could do anything I put my mind to. Once the musical opened, my life changed for the better. I became popular. Girls wanted to be with me all the time. Boys wanted to hang with me because I was the star of the show. I felt I had found my way, my path.

This period of my life took a pivotal turn. As a Seventh-day Adventist, I strictly observed the Sabbath. Friday night and Saturday daytime were reserved for religious endeavors, not secular activities, so performing in the musical on Friday night would be forbidden. If I chose to go into the entertainment business, this restriction would always be a problem.

The first Friday night performance approached. *What should I do?* At that time, I did not think I could go to my parents for guidance. After all, it was their religion: my father had converted from Catholicism to the Seventh-day Adventist Church, adopting my mother's faith, which set all the behavioral requirements for them and, by extension, my brother and me. Everyone knows religious converts are among the strictest regarding rules and dogma.

I decided to sneak out of the house Friday night and do the performance without my parents' knowledge because the theater was, after all, my newfound love. This one choice set in motion a series of events that led to my parents leaving the Black Seventh-day Adventist Church and moving to a more liberal white Seventh-day

Adventist Church. They put my needs and wishes above the dictates of their church. Probably more than anything else, my parents' support led me to decide to study music, dance, and theater in college. They continued to believe in me and consistently supported my decision to study the performing arts.

The test of that support came shortly after I had finished the run of the high school musical. When the elders of our church heard about what I had done and that I had even decided to study theater in college, they paid me a visit. I was at home one evening when I heard a knock on the door. To my surprise, three tall, middle-aged, overweight Black men dressed in dark suits—looking like the mob had sent them—leered at me from our doorstep.

My father answered the door. He greeted these intimidating men with a warm welcome and reverence. I, on the other hand, was scared of what they might say or do. After all, I was eighteen, old enough to think I was an adult and naive enough to be frightened of my own shadow. They pushed their way into the living room where I sat. I listened as they spoke with great force and conviction. I had learned from my limited theater training about projection in speaking from the stage. They obviously had learned that same lesson as well, perhaps from their religious training. The spokesperson of the ominous trio spoke first.

"We understand," he said, "that you are interested in the performing arts and are interested in pursuing that as a career. You should realize that that would be a tremendous mistake. That is a world of great temptations and unmentionable evils and would provide constant conflicts with your faith and religious beliefs." They did not realize I'd already decided to perform on the Sabbath.

"If you chose this lifestyle," the spokesperson said, "it could result in you having to leave the church. We are sure you would not want that to happen." I was stunned. *How could it be that I should have to make such a decision now?* I thought. *After all, there are musicians and performers also in the church. I see them singing and playing instruments on every Sabbath I attend. And during Christmas, there's the annual performance of Handel's* Messiah. *Numerous musicians and performers are always involved.*

By that time in my upbringing, I had come to believe I could be anything I wanted. I could make my way without giving up my spiritual life. I answered as respectfully as I could.

"I understand," I replied, "and I will consider all my options and the consequences of my career choices on my life and spiritual well-being. And I thank you for taking the time to counsel me. I will seriously think about all you've said."

Just as defiantly as they arrived, they glided to the front door, reminding us that they would see us at church that Saturday. They left with confidence that they'd made a most successful closing case and presentation.

After they'd gone, I turned my focus to my parents and heard the same comforting message from them: "Geoffrey, you can do and be whatever you want to be. Just be true to yourself." What words of inspiration!

I quickly discovered, however, that the attention that comes with being a popular person can turn negative in a heartbeat. For example, the following year, when I was cast as Sid Sorokin, the lead in *The Pajama Game*, the music coach invited me to her house for a one-on-one coaching session.

When I arrived, the odor of an unusual incense or perfume permeated the room. It was not at all a pleasant or inviting smell. *This is weird*, I thought. *Something strange is going on.* Nonetheless, I continued to get ready for a coaching session. My teacher, dressed in provocative attire, was in a peculiar yet casual mood. Instantly, she came very close to me, clearly invading my personal space. I immediately got uncomfortable.

"I will play the female role," she said, "and you should sing your part." Her perfume and the incense engendered feelings that I'd just stepped into a brothel of sorts. She was a very thin woman of some Hispanic heritage. I could not tell any more than that as she always wore a wig, which changed style or color every day or so, and dark glasses that made her look like some character out of a book I never wanted to read. She told me where I should begin my vocal passage, which was, curiously, just before the romantic scene. I sang. Reaching the part where I kiss the female co-lead, I paused, thinking, *She'll give me a staging note or two.*

"Go on," she said. "Kiss me." I realized she had intended our so-called rehearsal to be a make-out session. Trying hard not to show my discomfort, I hemmed and hawed and quickly made an excuse.

"I think I better go," I said. "My ride is waiting in the car outside, and I need to speak with her." This ride was my girlfriend, who had already cautioned me about going to a teacher's home after hours alone. I'd thought no teacher would ever take advantage of a student like that.

As my teacher puckered up for the kiss, I promptly left her house. I'd learned, once again, that I had better watch out for the teachers!

Another important aspect of my education, regardless of the discipline, was understanding that it comprised two components: theory and practice. I set myself to gather as much experience and practical training as possible. Unacknowledged guides or teachers often took me under their wings and became my "angels." I developed a particular liking for my speech teacher in high school, who was also trained in theater and directed the school's yearly onstage offerings. He was always encouraging and seemed to see more of my potential rather than my failures. I also found in one of the assistant principals in high school a person who became a wonderful support system, someone who I could go to and share my concerns and who would listen.

On one occasion, I saw him in the hallway. He said, "I want you to come to my office after your classes. I have something I want to share with you." I went to his office later that day, and he greeted me with a smile and offered me a seat. Sitting down, I wondered, *What did I do wrong this time?* To my surprise, he said, "I run a national program called Boys' Town. It is a program where students are selected from each state to come to Washington, DC, during the summer for two weeks. They live in the dorms on the campus of Georgetown University and study the makeup and workings of the federal government. They spend time on Capitol Hill and get to hear from legislators from all over the country. I would like you to consider representing the District of Columbia in this program. It is a lot of fun and work but a tremendous learning experience about the federal government. It will also give you an opportunity to see what it is like living in a dormitory on a college campus. Interested?"

I couldn't say yes fast enough. As it turned out, it became one of the highlights of my high school experiences. Boy, was it an exciting program, and I learned so very much. Just as he said, we lived in one of the Georgetown University dorms, ate in the dining halls, went to Capitol Hill every day, and spoke with actual legislators. We took the subway only for legislators, were greeted in spaces designated for Congress members, and had class lectures daily about government and its functions. It almost made me want to be a politician.

After graduating from high school, another such practical learning experience also occurred. It was the summer of 1964. It started like every other summer—sweltering hot and humid. I wanted a summer job, thinking it would be an effective transition to college, and I could pick up more spending money. In the library, I found what looked like the perfect opportunity in the arts section of the *National Register of Summer Jobs* for nonunion employees: "House Singer/MC" at the Old Stone Resort somewhere in the Pennsylvania mountains. I wrote a letter of application about my wonderful performing abilities.

Using the money I had saved, I had a headshot taken that, to this day, makes me look like an American Beatle. My hair was perfectly straightened and cut with even bangs across my large forehead. One afternoon, all these efforts paid off when I received a phone call from the owner of the resort.

Me in the summer of 1964 sporting my "Beatles look." That's the used tuxedo my parents loaned money to me to buy for my job as an MC at a summer resort.

"Is this Geoffrey Newman?" he said. "We have a problem inasmuch as our house singer left unexpectedly. We have an opening for this weekend. Would you be willing to come and perform for us this weekend?"

"Yes, of course," I replied.

When I told my parents about my new opportunity, they were hesitant. Yet, true to their unqualified support for my dreams, they agreed to let me go. I threw some clothes together and planned my three-hour drive to this beautiful location.

When I arrived at the resort, the beauty of that region surprised me. I inhaled the clear, clean air and the smell of fresh-cut grass. Though I arrived with no complications on the way, I was scared! I thought of myself as taking on yet another role—that of a celebrity, a nightclub singer. Yet I possessed little to no knowledge of what I was getting myself into. I checked in at the main entrance and was given my room and schedule for the weekend.

In anticipation of the job, I had purchased a "fake book," a collection of standard songs in basic keys that would give the accompanying piano player the musical outline of each song I sang. I was very good at hearing a key and reproducing the sound. Band, choir, and the high school musical had taught me how to read music, so I could "fake" it, just like the book.

I was a bit too arrogant and confident because, after all, I was the high school musical star. I would find out that my attitude was just what I needed to capitalize on this opportunity.

The club had arranged for me to meet the band or house orchestra (five or six players) for a sound check. At this rehearsal, we set sound levels, adjusted the keys, and agreed upon the entrances and endings of each tune we would perform. I adjusted the key and musical arrangements for each tune, trying, for the first time, to set my musical style. Surprisingly, all that went very well. I left and went back to my room.

The staff, including me, stayed in rooms away from the main hotel building, in the back of the property. I was to introduce the guest performers for the weekend and sing an occasional song.

As frightened as I was, excitement and adrenaline kept me ready for this new opportunity. The day went by quickly, and night was approaching. My moment was at hand. I had heard someone say that the more frightened you were, the better the performance would be. If only I could put all those feelings into the performance! I prayed this would work for me as every bone in my body shook.

When the audience was in place, the band started the agreed-upon introduction. My cue to enter arrived. I took a deep breath, submerged every ounce of fear, convinced myself these feelings were natural, and, as I had done not-so-many times in high school, strode onto the stage. Ironically, I felt extremely comfortable onstage. Once I got in front of the audience, something inside me took over. I was at home and at ease.

At the end of the Friday night performance, the resort hired me for the weekend for three performances. By the end of the weekend, I was hired for the rest of the summer. I was a professional nightclub singer. How cool! I drove back home at the end of the weekend to inform my parents and gather my stuff for the rest of the season.

The only problem that concerned me was that Saturday night was formal, and I would need a tuxedo. I went to my parents and explained that if they loaned me the money, I would pay them back from my earnings. They agreed. I bought a beautiful used black tux with bright, shiny black satin lapels. I looked like a younger version of Johnny Mathis, my mother's star celebrity. *How could I go wrong?* I thought. *I even look the part.* I needed to be back at the resort in three days, so there wasn't much time to get all my things together. I did it, though, and drove back to the Poconos with no problems.

Striving (1956–1964)

The gig was the beginning of my steady flirtation with the entertainment industry. That summer, however, I learned about the rigor needed to sustain high-end performances. The job also introduced me to a way of life I had only heard about. The after-hours crowds threw caution to the wind and partied like there was no tomorrow. The best performance work on the stage or in the club was all about being in control. Yet the resort was clearly a place where guests could lose complete control. I had always been blessed that this other side of performance, perhaps because I was raised as a Seventh-day Adventist, never captured or even drew my attention. But things were about to change.

That summer was significant, too, because I left the nest and tried things for myself—professionally, yes, but also personally. I met all kinds of people—musicians, dancers, singers, and even an ice-skating troupe of ice dancers and spinners. We were all provided housing, so before and after every show, someone hosted a party in their room. That summer, I learned to party, smoke a joint, and have sex with men and women.

One such learning experience revolved around the ice-skating performers. They were wild. I had never seen people drink and smoke as much as they did. Yet on a moment's notice, they could be ready for a performance. One such night, I participated in all the fun, thinking in my youthful ignorance that I could keep up with these veterans of the night. I couldn't, so I ran late for the nightly performance. Somehow, I made it backstage just in time, heard my musical cue, and ran out onto a special stage that had been set up for the ice dancers. In my rush, I forgot to don my special spiked shoes for walking on the ice. I slid right across the stage and plunged into the lap of a patron sitting in the front row. Fortunately, it was a female who seemed not at all upset to have the young, attractive MC sitting in her lap!

Of course, not to be embarrassed, I sang to this woman as if the move had all been planned. There were hoots of laughter and thunderous applause. Many times since then, I have learned how to go with the flow onstage and off, but that night, I learned to never, ever lose control at any time in any place if I was to be a successful professional performer. I could party as much as I wished, but I must always be ready to go onstage at a moment's notice.

These were early—or, as some would say, impressionable—years when I discovered that I was the protagonist of my own story, my unique play, my life. I realized that the scars I obtained during this period of my life came from both external as well as internal forces. Sure, it often appeared that I was a victim of what others initiated—government policies, teachers' anger or hate, and my parents' visions of my direction or future. Yet I realized I could forge my path. Through hard work and seeing challenges as opportunities to grow and get better, I controlled my destiny. I would not let forces stop me, limit my growth, and define my direction, my path. I came to realize that the dramatic action moving my life along from one experience to another, though filled with many obstacles along the way, was always under my control. I simply had to buckle down, shape my destiny, envision my future, overcome what others might think are my limitations, and continue to believe that it was always "better to cry now than be sorry later."

ACT 2

HIDING (1963-1974)

MY SEXUAL EDUCATION was a little more difficult to manage. In high school, I had an ongoing sexual relationship with a mixed-race, female, ethnic-looking student we'll call Monica. To maintain our relationship, it had to be in private, never in the open. As this high school was newly integrated, dating outside one's racial group was strictly forbidden, and that included mixed-race students. It was 1963, and parents didn't approve—students frowned, and teachers seemed to think of interracial dating on any level as bad behavior. To some degree, this attitude made our relationship even more exciting. Also, sex was such a strong temptation, I just had to experiment. My raging adolescent hormones often guided my actions much more than my reasoning. With Monica, I fell easily into a dual life: during the day, I flirted and acted like I was single. After school, Monica and I would find any excuse to hook up. We explored our sexual desires on a regular basis. We always gave into our sexual desires, urges, and seeming needs. We were young lovers, enjoying the pure innocence of young love and what that has to offer. Our sexual explorations led to what should have been an expected and most normal consequence: she became pregnant—a most difficult condition considering abortion was illegal at that time.

This is my high school graduation picture, taken in 1964 (pre-"Beatles look").

Fortunately, Monica was levelheaded and organized—a take-charge woman determined to keep control over her destiny, her own life, and her body. After much discussion, she took the lead in this situation. She sought information about medical reproductive services from a reliable friend and told me what the cover story was and what my role in it would be. I would need to cover half the cost of the procedure, which seemed only fair. A plan was designed. So on one rainy afternoon, she made an excuse to her parents that she was sleeping over with a group of her girlfriends, and I drove her to what seemed like an abandoned storefront. She got out of the car. We were both tense, very nervous, frightened and worried, yet we were resolved that what we were doing was the best decision for us both. However, as she stepped outside of my car, closed the door, and turned to leave, I knew that our lives would never be the same, and neither would our relationship. When the procedure was completed, she had one of her trusted girlfriends pick her up and take her back to the girlfriend's home, where she would recover before going home the next day. Afterward, my blame and shame became just too difficult to bear alone. I shared my dilemma with my mother. To my surprise, she was stern and clear about my lack of responsibility, but she was also understanding. I learned later in my life that she had endured similar circumstances with my brother and, eventually, even my father. Apparently, it was difficult for many males in my family to keep their zippers up and their pants on when it came to flirting with women. From then on, though, I always insisted on using prophylactics during sex. I had learned a very vital lesson the hard way.

However, my complicated teenage romance grew weaker and weaker. We stopped being lovers, drifted into a supportive friendship with a little anger thrown in the mix, and then lost contact entirely. Our experience caused us both enormous emotional scars and taught me there are consequences to every action—and that some are lifelong. I learned that losing control of your senses for a quick moment of satisfaction is not fair to either partner and that I had to think first of the consequences before engaging in any sexual act, particularly when procreation was possible. After the abortion, I never again took sex lightly, casually, or without thinking of the consequences of my actions.

I also grew from another experience in those Pennsylvania mountains. On those lush green mountaintops, I discovered a side of my sexuality I had never before experienced: sex with a man. I found a place of sexual satisfaction I hadn't known existed. In those days, however, sex with a man, particularly if you thought of yourself as bisexual, as I did back then, was done only "on the down-low," or privately. You went to hidden locations and arranged meetings in unusual, nontraditional meeting spots and unexpected places, often at spontaneous times. During that era, sex as a threesome—one man and two women or two men and one woman—was thought to be normal bohemian or free love and not at all as gay.

The term "gay" was not in my vocabulary. If I were to experience a gay lifestyle, I felt I had to settle for living that life behind closed doors. Surprisingly, that didn't seem all that difficult or unusual since I always had a text and a subtext in my life: the duplicity of living as a Black man in a white world. So I could be straight during the day and gay in the evening.

And, boy, did my gay life flourish and expand on those mountaintops! The female performers would continually hit on me. So did the men. There, I learned that being gay was not being effeminate; it was sharing emotions with another man in ways only a man could share with another man, a bonding of sorts. I discovered that I possessed a feminine and masculine side and that both could be included in my sexual life. I also came to understand that truly connecting and giving completely to another person, male or female, is what turned sex into love.

The summer also revealed another truth: a cover does not always reflect what's inside the book. A case in point was my summer fling with a man we'll call John, an Old Stone Resort staffer. He did handyman jobs around the property. John was my age, eighteen or nineteen, six feet two, and 185 pounds of solid muscle. He was a vision of what was later called a "hunk." Of non-white heritage, he looked like an ethnic version of Tarzan. I saw him around the club and pool area doing odd jobs. My gaze always sought him out in the crowd, though I somehow didn't know what that meant. One day, he looked back! My heart raced with anticipation and excitement. *Are my hormones getting the best of me?* But he did look as if I turned him on, too.

His steady, unwavering gaze suggested that I follow him. He wore a tight-fitting tank top pullover, which exposed his tanned, muscular arms. As he moved from one location to another, his muscles glistened from the sun. His pants were so low on his waist that my imagination made me desperately want to explore more. When he sauntered away, he looked back and caught my eye, silently bidding me to follow. And, boy, did I. I followed him to a space behind a shed where no one could see us, where we were completely isolated, where no one could discover or hear our liaison. We struck up a conversation, small talk at first, that quickly advanced to more intimate, sexually suggestive dialogue.

"It's hot out here," John said. "I'm sweaty. I need to change. My room is just over there. Wanna come and join me?"

"You lead the way," I answered.

We went to his room, which was not air-conditioned. By then, I was completely caught up in the moment. We rapidly undressed each other and, as if we were hired body inspectors, explored every inch of each other's bodies. Though that one hot scene was over in minutes, it seemed to last forever. The sex was like nothing I had ever experienced and satisfying far beyond anything I had ever encountered with Monica. I gave of myself completely and learned what it meant to be spent of emotion and sexual tension. In that small amount of time, I had changed. I had found my way. I smiled as I walked my new intimate friend back to my room, feeling I'd met a true traveling companion with whom I could share anything.

The resort did not provide air-conditioned rooms to any house staff, including the MC, and the day continued to be hot in more ways than one. Once we were inside my room, a small space with one window, a modest wardrobe, and a small bathroom, I was frightened, though captivated, by the big hunk of a stud who wanted me as much as I wanted him. Once again, he started undressing. *Yikes! Is this really happening?* We could not get enough of each other. The next hour was a lovemaking feast I will never forget.

Similar adventures filled my summer with John, but always in secret and never in public, much like I had masked my feelings for Monica at school. There was a difference, though. This time, I felt complete, as if I'd found my true nature. I'd found what I'd been waiting, even yearning, to experience.

That summer, I learned that bisexual men, as they were called back then, could act perfectly heterosexual during the day and very homosexual at night—the real meaning of "on the down-low." I also realized that there were very simple but hard-clad rules for this behavior: Never show emotion toward the same sex when meeting in public. You can be friendly and kind, but you cannot ever show any intimate connection with a same-sex partner if you don't want to be discovered. But you can be as intimate as you wish with an opposite-sex partner, even in public.

When I saw my new intimate friend during the day, I acted like we worked at the same place but had nothing in common. Eventually, we allowed people to think we were good friends. After being intimate with me in his off-hours, my friend would go home to his live-in girlfriend and, once again, be straight. This pattern continued throughout the summer. I lived two lives, completely different from one another, while internally hiding great and passionate emotions. I decided to keep this secret life to myself, not sharing it with anyone, even my parents or brother. I rationalized that this choice—to keep this part of me exclusively private—could work if I could truly control my feelings. I felt that losing control was a no-no.

To me, this reality became the show business world. From then on, I had a public persona and a private persona, and I would try never to let these two worlds come together or even cross paths. This approach seemed to work. Throughout the rest of my life, I found that many others, particularly performers, embraced this philosophy of duality. When I went off to college in Ohio, I continued to keep my two worlds apart but lived each to the fullest: Black man acting white; gay man acting straight.

Wanting to expand its size, Ashland College admitted more than double its previous numbers for the 1964 first-year students. Dormitory space was insufficient, so many in my class had to live in off-campus housing. In my second semester, I was one of the freshmen set adrift off campus. My first semester, however, was what most college-bound students experienced: I was brought to campus, dropped off by my parents, and expected to swim, not sink, in these strange, unfamiliar seas.

After my parents headed home, I was on this strange campus, standing alone with no friends, wondering what I should do and where I should go. I met a similarly frightened freshman whose parents had just dropped him off. He, too, was looking to explore this unfamiliar world. While we walked along a beautiful campus street, a car of guys pulled up.

"Want to come to our frat house?" one asked. "We're having a rush party, and ours is the best."

I didn't know what a rush party was. *What a wonderful experience,*

I thought. *This isn't going to be too bad. I can easily make friends here.* Or so it appeared. As I looked around campus, I saw not one other Black face. Panic grabbed my gut, but I subdued it. *This is just like the Poconos.* That experience had started out frightening but, in the end, proved positive. Exciting experiences had taught me to take a more trusting approach to new encounters. I decided to go with the flow and let my instincts guide the way.

That rush party fraternity turned out to be embarrassing. I walked into a pretty traditional-looking room, something like that in a fifties clubhouse. Guys were standing around welcoming guests, ready to give the story of their fraternity, their history, why this house was better than the others. However, no one ever spoke to me. They talked to my new first-year friends but acted like I was not even there. I felt ignored—unwanted. I would not have been surprised if someone had shown me to the kitchen or handed me a broom. It didn't take long for me to get the message, and I said, "I think I need to get back to the dorm and unpack." As no words were expressed to the contrary, I left and noticed the tension on some faces, relieved that I had not created a scene or made any trouble. Clearly, I was not welcomed.

In the end, I was blackballed from becoming a pledge. Some members of the fraternity were not ready to accept a Black boy as one of their brothers.

I met three kinds of people: those who hated me because of my ethnicity; those who thought I wasn't Black enough because I wasn't an athlete, didn't speak in Black slang, and didn't exhibit street behavior from the Black ghetto; and those who appeared to like me and found my Heinz 57 cultural fusion exotic, perhaps even intriguing. The latter became my friends. I became very close to some of my fellow students and developed strong friendships. However, the first two groups of people often created a very hostile environment. I rarely felt comfortable and at ease. I had to watch where I went, managing never to be alone and always with a group of fellow students. My newfound love for music, dance, and theater meant I was the solo voice in the choir singing the Negro spiritual and portraying the servant in the college play. I thought, *I am not going to become a star or celebrity here.*

I rarely felt like I could be a relaxed, carefree guy who didn't have to choose his words very carefully, speaking in standard English when in white settings and in Black English when around people of color from the community.

I learned to be very cautious of those around me, particularly those with the potential or intention to harm me. The school provided no measure of support in that regard. I was on my own. I quickly learned that if I thought of myself as alone, I would ultimately depend on my resources to get me through all precarious or problematic situations.

I needed to hone my powers of persuasion and logic and find other ways to vent my artistic side. This approach—talking my way out of tight situations or into an opportunity—seemed to work much better than forcing an obstacle out of the way. In fact, this simple approach of trying to understand the opposing point of view led to my studying subjects such as philosophy and logic. If I could better understand human behavior, I would have a better chance of achieving personal success regardless of the circumstances or the obstacles.

My home environment had been what many new friends and acquaintances called loud and argumentative. My mother was always loudly debating my father, and my brother was always loudly debating both our parents. I would always try to get a word in edgewise. When I brought new friends home, they never failed to comment on how my family seemed to argue a lot. I always explained that we were not seriously attacking each other; we simply liked to debate aggressively. This was my family's way of discussing issues. If you could not win the debate, you lost the right to hold your position.

This home training helped me navigate many currents in school and life. It gave me the confidence to go into any situation, take control, and make my case. When I was a high school junior, I decided to enter an oratory contest with two components: a prepared speech and extemporaneous speaking. After writing the speech for hours, I took it to my father, who edited it until it sounded like a presidential address. Then, he coached me until I sounded like a professional. For me, the extemporaneous part was just another night at the dinner table. I won that competition because my family had taught me to think and respond rapidly.

On one hand, winning was very rewarding. On the other, it seemed perfectly natural. The win empowered me to believe that, once again, I could compete on my feet. I had the gift of gab and could talk my way into or out of any situation.

But talk alone would not be enough to rectify the situation I faced at Ashland College. Each day, I felt trapped. If I stayed, I would play servant roles or boy-next-door characters in poorly written plays. I would never be given the lead. When it appeared that my future would be nothing but dismal, I contacted my father and explained my case and my feelings. I'd thought he might be disappointed in me, but no. The first words out of his mouth were, "You need to come home and go to Howard University."

My father had just been appointed director of personnel at Howard. Previously, as director of its computer center, he had updated the university's academic and personnel records, converting them to an efficient online system. I asked my father if I should leave after that semester, my third at Ashland College, and come home after the Christmas break.

"Yes, I'll make the arrangements at Howard," he said, "and you can transfer immediately." That sounded perfect to me. I could hardly wait. Fortunately, my parents had given me a car to drive to Ohio when I started my sophomore year.

I did have several concerns. For one, I had never, since the fourth grade, gone to a Black school, and Howard was the mecca for Black education. Given my struggles at Ashland, though, I welcomed the change. I would only have to fight for the performing roles, not the opportunities. *Perhaps the lessons of how to live as a Black man in a white world will be easier there?*

My mother and me—my father took this photo when they dropped me off at Ashland College at the beginning of my sophomore year. That little light blue Volkswagen Beetle on the right is the car they gave me.

My move from Ashland in Ohio to Howard in Washington, DC, was an enlightening and surprisingly eventful learning experience in itself. I had packed all my personal belongings into my cute VW Bug, expecting to travel without incident, as I had twice before. As I got in my trusty little Volkswagen, I realized I'd filled every inch of the vehicle with everything I had collected over the past year and a half. The quantity of my stuff left me only a tiny hole of visibility through my back window. That seemed okay, though, as it was a beautiful December day. I had checked the weather forecast, and it appeared to be clear driving all the way.

I said my goodbyes, surprised at how many people I had befriended during my three semesters at Ashland and even more moved by how my leaving affected them. As I drove away, a sadness came over me. Yet I was not really unhappy or distressed but rather extremely excited. After all, I was about to start a new chapter in my life, one where I could flourish in acting, music, and performing. I had called my parents to let them know I was on my way and started to drive out of town, expecting the journey to take six to eight hours.

As I drove through the campus, I passed the row of beautiful fraternity houses, remembering the parties I was invited to and the day I was blackballed from membership because I was Black. I was transferring to a school where my skin color would not make one bit of difference to my success. I'd make friends, learn, grow as an artist, and find my place in a performing arts career. Besides, Howard was known for developing Black artists who became stars. I wanted to be one of those individuals. So I resolved that I was on my way to achieving great success.

I drove through Ohio and then onto the Pennsylvania Turnpike, which was always the most challenging part of the drive as the weather could change in a second—and that is what happened. Snow fell lightly at first and then got worse as I pressed forward. It was as if nature did not want this journey to be easy. Maybe it was payback for assuming my life would immediately become better. Before long, I could barely see the road, much less the cars in front of me. As I drove, the storm's ferocity kicked into high gear with more snow and high winds. *What have I possibly done to deserve this?*

How ironic! I was fighting to leave an all-white school, then fighting through a white snowstorm. I kept reminding myself I was used to handling unexpected circumstances, particularly negative ones. So I decided to stay the course and not panic. When I could not even see ahead, I decided to get off at the next exit ramp and wait until the roads were plowed. I'd call home and let my parents know I would be considerably later than planned. I did just that.

With the time difference, I woke them up with the bad news. To my surprise, they appeared to be more panicked than I was. My mother got on the phone first.

"How bad is it?" she asked. "What do you plan to do?"

I said I'd gotten a room in the nearest motel and thought I'd wait out the storm before returning to the highway and resuming my trip. My mother thought that was a good plan. My father then got on the phone.

"Where are you *exactly*?" he asked. I examined the road map I'd bought when I first made this trip and pinpointed my location. "Just sit tight, get some rest, and keep in touch."

Sounded good to me. I was tired from the intensity of the drive, so I fell right asleep. Two hours later, the phone on my bedside table rang. It was my mother.

"Your father is on his way to help you with the rest of the drive," she said. "He booked an airline ticket." He would meet me at a nearby airport. My mother gave me my father's plane arrival information and said he had already left for the airport. I hung up the phone and packed my things.

My little car was so packed with personal belongings that I had no idea where my father would sit. The passenger seat was filled. I went to the car and dumped anything I considered nonessential into the trash. Most of these items were tidbits from athletic events or party favors from going out with friends. I redistributed everything, emptying the passenger seat so there was just enough room for my father to sit with several items on his lap.

I checked out of the motel and made my way to the airport. Pulling up to the main terminal, I saw my father standing in front, looking for me. I pulled up to where he was standing. He walked over to the driver's side.

"Why don't you sit in the passenger seat, and I will take the first shift of driving?" he asked.

Of course, all those items that would have been on my father's lap were now on mine, and I realized just how uncomfortable this position really was.

I thanked him for coming, feeling a little embarrassed I had caused him so much trouble. I assured him I could have made the remaining drive and that he really didn't need to go to such an enormous effort and expense. He said he felt better if he was with me rather than sitting at home wondering if I was all right or in danger. That was just my parents' way. Anything they could do to help me they would not hesitate to do.

I realized then I was and never would really be alone. Loving parents who put my needs even above their own always had my back. At that moment, I had the confidence of a bull. Nothing could stop me.

As it turned out, my father drove the entire way. During the drive, we had private time to have many father-and-son discussions. We were rarely in a situation where he and I could talk to each other without others hearing the conversation. So this became a uniquely rare opportunity. He told me about how excited he and my mother were about my moving back home. I could get remission of tuition thanks to his job at Howard, so they could give me an increase in my spending allowance. They would even pay for me to share an apartment off campus if I wished. All I needed to do was tell them what I desired. More importantly, he took this time, alone in the car with me, to build up my spirits and self-confidence. He told me how proud they were of me and how, once again, I could be and become whatever I chose to do in life. I was the master of my own fate, and they would support me, whatever I chose to do or how I chose to live. They would always be my rock. I could always rely on them if ever I was in any need. There was nothing I could not share with them. They were my foundation. By the time we arrived back home, I had forgotten the perilous journey we had endured, the snowstorm we had overcome. I only felt their love and support—and my own eagerness to begin a new chapter of my life.

Black students from all over the world flocked to Howard, which had been established after the Civil War, to educate formerly enslaved people. Its philosophy was to prepare the Black student to achieve success in a white world. My time there was even more exciting and unpredictable than I could have ever hoped for. The year was 1966, and student protests were erupting on most major college campuses. Howard was no exception: there were student protests and sit-ins just about every day. The Student Nonviolent Coordinating Committee had taken the Howard administration by storm. These demonstrations protesting segregation against African Americans were part of the Civil Rights Movement that had started in the South.

I joined the drama department at Howard. Part of the curriculum was producing plays. My fellow students and I had little to no time to engage in the protest demonstrations. I think the faculty felt that the busier they could keep the students, the fewer political demonstrations they would have to deal with. If we were not in class, we were onstage performing or backstage running a performance. Initially, this plan seemed to work well for the faculty. After Martin Luther King Jr. was killed in 1968, Washington, DC, was on fire, and the national scene exploded. There were riots in the streets and police, it seemed, on every corner. When I drove back and forth to class, I often used my acting abilities to let the rioters know, as much as possible, that I supported their protest movement. I also avoided the police by looking like I was a college student, not part of the street violence. I always watched what was happening around me, in or out of the car. When I saw people in the streets yelling, "We shall overcome. Hang in there," I would hang my free hand out the window to show support.

Every day, I had to move through or around violence, angry people, and just unhappy circumstances. By the time I advanced to the end of my senior year, the situation had worsened so much that each day, I would arrive at school and first look for a posting to see whether my class was being held or whether a bomb threat had closed down the building or campus again. In every community, Blacks and whites lived in a constant state of tension. More importantly, though, and because of the student protest movement, all Americans were forced to face the degrading conditions and enormous struggles of being Black in an often-hostile white world and the reality of police brutality everywhere.

Hiding (1963–1974)

One night, when the department was performing James Baldwin's drama, *Blues for Mister Charlie*, based on the 1955 murder of fourteen-year-old Emmett Till in Mississippi, I experienced an epiphany. I was working backstage when a group of about four Black students stormed the stage and told all the white people to leave the theater immediately.

"Get out now," they yelled, "if you know what's good for you!" The audience rushed to the front door. Of course, I agreed with the protest movement. I had been a victim of discrimination many times, but these students were ready for war. I was frightened. *What must they think of us?* I thought. *Here we are putting on a play, entertaining people. Will they think we are part of the problem?*

Fortunately, these students embraced us as part of their movement. We were one because James Baldwin was heralded as an outspoken, bold Black writer spreading a message of overcoming oppression. Still, there was fear—not from the students protesting but from a society that didn't want to hear from us at all, from a society that believed Black voices should be marginalized or completely silenced. Questions filled my mind: *What would happen if the white society was successful? What kind of a world was I about to enter as an adult, as an artist? How could I flourish when so many others were forced to fail? How could I share my talents without compromising my beliefs? Is that even possible?* Those and many more questions clouded my mind.

Suddenly, the precarious position of a Black man in a white world came into even sharper focus for me. Until then, I had painfully understood how my Black skin affected my personal, academic, and professional life, but that night, I began to understand that my situation—and the situation of all Black people in the United States—was the same: in a state of turmoil. I saw that even as a mere student, I could not escape the Black anger, white fear, unrest, the rage of the civil rights struggle. I realized that if one person was not free of discrimination, no one was, regardless of the color of their skin, their background, or their economic status.

Those students who stormed the stage were expressing hate, and I remembered how hate could destroy. I recalled my days in the public-school system, how so many negative experiences so angered me that I began to hate everything and everyone. I remembered how that hate almost took over my entire life. It would have almost consumed me entirely if I had let it. To better myself, I had to reach for hope and optimism; I had to focus on joy and my love for exploring what I did not know. I could not allow hate to become a distraction. I could not lose my focus. I became resolved never to let that happen to me. I would never let hate of any kind define who I am, who I am becoming, or who I want to be.

In spite of the campus unrest, I made it to every scheduled class that year and achieved a 4.0 grade point average, or all *A*s, in my drama courses. In fact, I won the Most Outstanding Student in Drama Award, given to the top graduating senior each year. I had been so successful in my studies at Howard that the chairman of the drama department held a graduation party at his home for me and gave me glowing letters of recommendation I could show to leading figures in the theater industry. I know this award and graduating with such high praise should have made me happy, even content and satisfied, but how could I be, considering the turmoil in the country and everyone's life around me? The depressing and confusing times made receiving any award rather irrelevant to me.

The enormous personal growth and self-respect I gained from the Civil Rights Movement enhanced my learning experiences at Howard University, which went far beyond the academic courses I had taken or the techniques and history I had learned. Because of the school's training program, coupled with the faculty's loving support, I understood my need to express myself as a unique individual and to commit to fostering and supporting social justice. I gained the strength to openly explore my creative potential and never apologize for my choices. I learned to take pride in who I am, what I am, and everything I hoped to be. I gained the self-confidence to face the many obstacles ahead and confront my fears, never hesitating to plan strategies to overcome the unknown or the unexpected. I learned social tools, acquired sensitivities, and developed an empathy for others that has guided me throughout my life.

At Howard, I was not only taught solid performance techniques but also how to find my unique voice. I learned how to be a Black man in any performance venue without relinquishing those aspects of my personality and ethnic background that were particular to me. I also learned how to use these gifts to bring the characters to life for me and the audience. For example, when I was mastering various roles in Shakespeare's plays, I channeled my background into the portrayal of those characters: the importance of family in the Black community, the competitiveness common to siblings in the Black family structure, the influence and strength of the Black church in forming and guiding behavior and developing cultural codes and customs.

I was taught how these elements from my own life were easily seen in the backgrounds of Elizabethan characters and their situations. This critical training enabled me, as a Black actor, to portray a wide variety of characters in a realistic manner. After a time, I believed I could understand and create any character by digging into my own experience to uncover universal points of intersection that would inform my interpretation. In so many ways, these historic and far-different-from-me characters became familiar as I found that their fears, hopes, and dreams resonated with my life and community. I learned to appreciate my gifts but never assume I was better than others. I thought of myself as a small part of "everyman." My hopes, dreams, fears, and anxieties were just like those of everyone. Those similarities enabled me to see myself as part of a bigger picture. In this world, all people are connected in their need to express themselves, live without regret, overcome fear, and create a reality that defines a future of joy, satisfaction, and even love.

The process sounds simplistic, but mastering this acting technique was far from a smooth ride. All actors, even lowly students, must deal with the personal and societal issues and pressures that swirl around our heads. The times after my Howard experiences were troubled, even turbulent. These were war times. To the outside world, students' desire to grow and learn was not a high priority. War games, political posturing, and using any efforts to destroy one's opponent became this country's behavior and goal.

Every day, there seemed to be political turmoil in the United States and around the world. In 1968, young men my age and older were called to serve in the army. My friends and I saw the draft as a possible end to our very lives. The fear of being drafted became an albatross around every young man's neck, a noose that seemed to get tighter each day we were alive. We were all torn about how to respond to the draft. One close friend left for Canada; I never heard from him again. Those I knew who had served and returned seemed tortured by what they had seen and endured just to stay alive. *How can war ever be good for solving a conflict?* I continued to think. *There must be better solutions than physically attacking each other—solutions that don't destroy people's lives.* This hope I continued to believe.

Hiding (1963–1974)

My number was 138 out of 366, so I lived under the pressure that I would eventually have to go. Being a conscientious objector was not enough to keep you from being called up to serve. This constant threat also awakened in me an intense appreciation for life. I began to value each day as if it were a lifetime.

I'd gotten a college deferment, but graduation would end that. I thought about graduate school to continue my deferment and about a big summer adventure that could provide a different sort of education. After all, it could be my last.

My parents, proud as they could be that one of their sons had gotten a college degree, and from Howard University no less, asked what I wanted as a graduation gift. It took me maybe two minutes to decide.

"I want a round-trip ticket to Europe," I said. By then, my parents were never surprised by what came out of my mouth. They gave me that ticket to the most exciting, inspiring adventure of my young lifetime.

Prior to going to Europe, I met with a friend from Ashland College and shared my plans: Europe for the summer, possibly graduate school in the fall if I wasn't drafted. Gary had already applied to what he touted as the best graduate theater training program in the country, Wayne State University.

"You study during the day," he said, "and perform at night." The day started in the late morning. No classes began for company members before 10 a.m.

The Hilberry Classic Repertory Theatre at Wayne State was a performance training graduate program for students earning a master's or doctorate. Each term presented eight different productions in rotation or repertory. The approach, which was to learn through doing, made this program one of the best worldwide. The company worked on every aspect of the production, from the box office to the stage and backstage. Each year, new students would be selected to replace those leaving the program. Two new productions would be added to the eight-show lineup while two others would drop out of the repertoire. Among Wayne State's distinguished graduates around that time were the comedienne, writer, and actress Lily Tomlin and Jeffrey Tambor. Years later, other graduates, such as Thorsten Kaye, David Ramsey, S. Epatha Merkerson, Tom Sizemore, Max Wright, and Erick Devine, finished that same program. Boy, was I intrigued! However, getting into this program would be difficult, and keeping up with its vigorous curriculum would be even harder. Gary and I continued drinking and talking about how much fun it would be to study and perform together.

Before Wayne State University's program came up, I already recognized that my talent and passion were more in directing than acting. I had graduated from Howard with majors in both. My strong debate background at home made me think that working as an actor would not make me happy. After all, a director would always tell me what to do, say, and feel. If I was going to be in the theater world, I decided I needed to be behind the scenes as a director, in control of the process, so I could use my artistic vision to establish all the "conventions," or guidelines, for a particular production.

In every theatrical production, the accumulated effect of the casting, staging, lighting, costuming, and even publicity builds to a particular message to the audience. If the audience puts aside logical reality and accepts what they see on the stage as real—the willing suspension of disbelief—they will be transported to another place and time, as defined by an artistic director's vision. That was exactly what I wanted to be: the artistic director, the inspirational leader, the guide for the entire theatrical experience.

The next period in my life seemed to be falling into place. I knew how I wanted to make my mark in this world. Directing—working with others, sometimes being the leader, and, more often, following others' leads—taught me more about myself than I could ever learn in a classroom setting. My godmother, Alma Blackmon, was the head of music for the general conference. She directed the choir for the Seventh-day Adventist Church; taught piano; helped open a new restaurant, the Tivoli, for the bar Mr. Henry's in Georgetown; and introduced Roberta Flack, one of her piano students, to the venue's owner, Henry Yaffe, who featured her in his new venture on Capitol Hill, from which Roberta became a star. Alma was the consummate director. She created special programs and concerts and featured singers and professional artists, such as Joyce Bryant, all as the director and coordinator, enabling gifted artists to find and feature their unique talents. She was my inspiration for what a director could be, an enabler for great artists' moments to surface.

I decided to take the risk and explore my talents through graduate school at Wayne State University. This move would also give me another draft deferment, but truly, I was far more excited about how I might learn and grow as an artist there. I knew I'd be stretching, perhaps further than I could even imagine, but my father's mantra echoed in my mind: "The greater the risk, the greater the return." This training could set in motion a course that could profoundly shape my personal and professional goals.

But first, I was off for a magical summer in Europe, where I could learn so many new and exciting things, hopefully far beyond my expectations.

Yes, this would be a whirlwind of a trip, an amazing experience for 1968. Thinking it might be a last hurrah, so to speak, I wanted to maximize the adventure. I came up with a great idea that some might call crazy: I would create a performance tour through Europe.

George and me in Europe in 1968 on our troubadour tour. We traveled all over Europe in that little Renault Quatre.

I reasoned that I could plan most of the details before I left the United States: countries I could visit, strategies for finding performance venues, and music I could prepare. My parents had agreed to give me some money along with this gift of a European airline ticket, so I had a small budget. What I didn't have was a partner, someone who could provide companionship, support, and perhaps another voice that would blend with my own, someone who wouldn't think my idea was absolutely foolish.

I recalled George, a friend from my high school days who played guitar and sang. Though we had never attended the same public high school, we had met at a party in Washington, DC. He had pulled out his guitar and started to play and sing, and I had joined in, harmonizing with him. People complimented our sound. He was a marvel on guitar, and his booming voice matched mine perfectly. We had both fallen in love with the folk music of the times. Throughout my college days, George and I had never lost track of each other. Whenever possible, we'd meet to create music together.

I thought he would be the perfect person to help me develop my idea, put the musical arrangements together, and plan the tour experience. I approached him and suggested we form a singing duo, much like a Peter, Paul, and Mary–type act, only without a Mary. The idea excited him, too. After a lot of persuasion, his parents agreed to fund him. Before I knew it, we were rehearsing songs and developing duets, vocal runs, and harmonies. George was my height and build, only white. He had straight black hair and looked much like a hippie. More importantly, though, he possessed a vibrant personality that exuded from his music. When we performed together, we looked like brothers from a different mother but of the same class, training, temperament, ambition, and background. We came to think of each other as brothers traveling down the road of life together, helping each other conquer the unknown.

When we sang together, it was magic. We were unbeatable. Our cares and even the world's problems yielded to the thrill of our innocent voices. We touched people with our singing and shared messages of protest, hope, inspiration, and love. Once we were ready to leave on tour, even our parents were convinced we had achieved something very special through song. I began to believe the trip was not as much a risk as an opportunity to deliver a needed message in those turbulent times. We would sing. We would help change the world. As the song said, "We Shall Overcome," and we did, time and time again.

Having planned our trip with the book *Europe on Five Dollars a Day*, we first flew to London and went to Piccadilly Circus—the first test of our plan. We stood on an empty street corner as people bustled around us. Everyone seemed to have a destination. Wherever they were headed, they were going there in a hurry. The air was filled with street noises and the smells of vendors cooking their enticing treats and specialties. We'd have to compete with them and other peddlers hawking their wares, selling papers, and announcing upcoming events. George and I looked at each other. *This is not going to be easy*. But we believed in the power of our sound.

George opened his guitar case and started playing our booming first song, "The Times They Are A-Changin'." As we had hoped, people stopped, listened, and reacted. Crowds gathered. Spontaneous applause erupted. Every song we sang garnered a bigger and bigger audience response. The opened guitar case began to fill with money and then more money. Passersby wanted to know where we were from and whether we had ever recorded. They praised our musicianship and asked where we were performing in town. All sorts of people stopped to listen—the young, the older, the affluent, students, parents with their children. Before we knew it, we had garnered a following, a welcoming audience, a cheering crowd.

George and I performed on that street corner for two nights before we were given a lead for a club that featured folk music groups. The club was willing to audition us, and just like that, we were booked for three nights. We were already an opening act in a nightclub!

After our success in London, we took a train to Edinburgh, Scotland, where we performed on the famed Princes Street across from Edinburgh Castle. The day was clear, the weather warm, and the people were extremely responsive and appreciative. That night, we were invited to stay in the home of one of our newfound fans, who treated us like one of their family members.

Day and night, our performances drew new admirers and supporters. Our folk music sound was fascinating, and being a Black and white duo of handsome young men from America added to the visual interest. The more we performed, the better we got, and the more audiences responded enthusiastically. And the more the audiences responded, the more confident we became. We were the Beatles from America, only singing protest music of change and hope.

Next, we flew to Brussels and picked up a Renault Quatre based on a lease-to-purchase agreement. We had made the arrangements and obtained international driver's licenses before we left the States. The Renault had a huge stick shift protruding from the middle of the dashboard. Luckily, we both knew how to drive a standard transmission. It looked a little strange, but in truth, everything looked odd to us young, inexperienced Americans—and that made the trip even more wonderful.

In England and Scotland, we could speak the language. To find our way in Belgium, we had to rely even more on our music and the friends it attracted. Once again, we followed the plan: we started on the street, auditioned for the owner of a local club, and got booked for a brief run. If we suggested to a club owner that we do the first performance just for tips, we never failed to get the gig. Our high adrenaline and excitement about being in Europe and our success winning the hearts of our audiences built so that it seemed like we had advanced press in the next town and the next. People expected us. We had little fear of failure because we could rely on each other. And we never failed to find someone in each town who would adopt us.

Young people our age responded to our music. They eagerly gathered around us, asking questions about the United States, the

Vietnam War, and our journey. We sometimes felt like US ambassadors representing our country with our little traveling show. Our European encounters helped us develop a deeper understanding of humanity: our differences were a strength, and strong similarities connected all people. We learned that fearing what appears to be different is a great mistake. Time and time again, we found that people who did not look or speak like us, people with dissimilar customs and behaviors, opened their homes to us with little to no hesitation.

From Amsterdam, we traveled to Paris, where street musicians and various performers were on every corner. But once again, we found a vacant sidewalk space, set up our little mobile sound system, put out our guitar case to receive donations, and sang our hearts out. We never performed in a traditional nightclub in Paris, but we made more money on the street there than anywhere else we performed. Before we knew it, we realized we had made more money than we started with and began to believe we could do this for months on end.

We became known as folk singers, troubadours traveling throughout Europe singing songs of peace, freedom, and love. It did not seem to matter if we were tall or short, Black or white, gay or straight, fat or thin. It only mattered that we treated others with loving respect and acceptance, as we hoped they would treat us.

We moved from Paris through the lush green countryside of the Pyrenees mountains to the Costa Brava in Catalonia, Spain. Our copy of *Europe on Five Dollars a Day* directed us to very inexpensive rooms in a fifth-century castle. As we pulled up to it, George and I felt we had been dropped into medieval history. The place exuded magic and mystical times. Its walls were made of the original stone—thick blocks of ancient sandstone and quartz carved to fit together perfectly. I could imagine wearing a different wardrobe, not jeans and a T-shirt, and following period customs and behaviors. I imagined street vendors of old and Elizabethan street markets right there.

"Disney would have a field day lighting and bringing this place to life," I told George.

Inside, the castle hallways looked like scenes from *Romeo and Juliet*. From our top-floor room, which also appeared not to have been touched by time, we saw a quaint town that reminded us of historic Europe. We, however, just seemed out of place. So did the tourists moving through the uneven, rustic, cobblestoned streets.

What a joyous feeling, though, to drink local wine and eat locally made cheeses while gazing at the beautiful Mediterranean waters. The trip seemed to be one big amazing dream. But it was not. Instead, it was one unexpected adventure after another. One day, we ventured onto the roof of this magnificent structure, silently using our eyes as cameras to capture every scene, venue, and visual composition. In my head, I could practically hear the shutters of each image being clicked and stored in my memory. We never wanted to forget these precious moments.

Sleeping in this historic place, however, was not at all comfortable, easy, or luxurious, but it was so extraordinary that the inconveniences simply did not matter. Living history superseded all else.

We drove around the coast of the Spanish Riviera to Nice on the French Riviera, where we were surprised to see the beaches covered with stones! There was no sand to be found. Yet people would put towels down on the rocks to take in the sun, giving the impression that they were as content as if they were sinking into the sand. We had made so much money by that time that we didn't feel the need to perform to pay our expenses. So we partied, drank, and partied some more and tried to blend in with the environment and not look like tourists.

From Nice, we continued around the Mediterranean coast into Italy and eventually ended up in Rome, stopping in Pisa, Florence, Venice, and many small towns along the way. Whenever there appeared to be a place for us to stop and perform, we did. But by that time of the tour, we were exhausted from all the driving and traveling, so we did more sightseeing than performing. We had picnics, met new people, and heard wonderful stories that many tourists would miss unless they rented a car. We also enjoyed breaking bread and sharing wine with the local natives.

From Italy, we drove north and into Switzerland, where we found a welcoming nightclub in the village of St. Gallen. After the first evening of performance, a Swiss family took us to their gasthaus, the equivalent of an American bed and breakfast, where we stayed and lived for almost a week. It was beautifully situated in the Swiss Alps, reminiscent of a scene from the *Sound of Music*. I could have stayed there forever. These were indeed magical times. I never wanted them to end.

While we were in Europe having the time of our lives, I got a telephone call from home. My mother informed me that I had been given an audition for Wayne State University's graduate program. I couldn't believe it! I had been called for an interview. Since I had applied as a directing major, more emphasis would be put on the interview than any other admissions criteria. This reality heartened me because performing had become very easy for me. If I thought of the interview as a performance, I was golden. After all, I had just concluded a three-month summer season as a successful nightclub singer, loved by audiences across Europe. I made plans to return home and prepare for the interview.

Reluctantly, George and I left Switzerland and headed north toward Brussels, where we turned over the car back to the dealership.

Every aspect of this trip had been wonderful, from the little odd lease-to-purchase automobile that looked like something from the circus to the gracious, generous people we met along the way. We probably took too many unnecessary risks, trusted too many strangers, and believed we could adapt to too many unpredictable situations. I am sure if our parents had known how we were living, we would have been summoned home immediately.

We hoped our European experience would be the first of many more international experiences. At that point, though, I had to say a sad and difficult farewell to George, who had become closer to me than my brother, and brought an end to my budding performing career. Boy, was this a downer. They say that the higher the flight, the greater the fall. And this was one huge letdown. I felt the choice of returning home was closing a door that I had just cracked open but had so many more possibilities I couldn't even fully imagine and would never explore. I was forced to stop dreaming and become an adult, like everybody else.

Since I was not from Detroit, my interview would be held off campus at Carnegie Mellon University in Pittsburgh. I managed to get to the correct location a little ahead of my interview time. As I waited in the hallway for my name to be called, I talked to another attractive, distinguished young man who was also waiting. His beautiful smile and crystal blue eyes seemed to invite me to incredible intimacy. Within minutes, he had moved the conversation to my returning to his room after my interview. Even though that's exactly how my wonderful summer fling had transpired in the Pennsylvania mountains, I was not experienced in handling this kind of invitation. While it intrigued me, I focused on getting through the interview and audition process. As my father would say, "Never lose sight of your objective, your goal."

"Maybe another time," I answered. That seemed to be the gentlest way of handling a come-on—a rejection that communicated reluctance to say no and possibly create hurt feelings.

Fortunately, at that very moment, my name was called. I walked into the room like the star had just arrived. After all, I'd just been approached by a stranger who thought I was the cat's meow. *Why wouldn't they want me?* Afterward, I felt that the interview had really gone well. I answered all their questions with poise and confidence and displayed a bravado that I hoped communicated that I had the skills to make them proud if I became one of their students. You never know what auditioners are truly thinking, though. Sometimes, too much confidence can be interpreted as arrogance, and that can sink the ship. This time, however, my senses were right.

About a week later, I got a phone call from Wayne State inviting me to join the company and pursue my master's degree at the same time. They also were pleased to offer me a full scholarship and yearly stipend. I just couldn't believe this was happening! Not only did I get admitted, but I also got a scholarship to one of the most highly competitive programs in the country. *My God, this is wonderful*, I thought. *I can maybe get a performing job in Detroit while going to school, and if possible, launch a career as a professional actor/director/singer while completing my degree.* Ambitious goals, to be sure, but the greater the risk, the greater the return. By then, though, the federal government had eliminated the draft deferment for graduate school students. I got ready to move to Detroit, praying I would not be drafted and forced to abandon this educational experience.

Studying at Wayne State provided mixed blessings. Though one of the best schools in the country, it was in a part of the city that was anything but safe, and the winters were the most brutal I had ever experienced. I could not believe people were expected to move through this frigid environment, arrive at work or school on time, and be ready and able to function on all cylinders. For me, each day was a struggle to conquer the weather, face the desperate homeless population, and arrive at my desired destination with a positive, creative attitude, prepared to explore my artistic potential. I would get to class or a performance without time to think or relax and try to focus, warm up, and perform whatever tasks were assigned. As this field of study was close to my heart, I was highly motivated to overcome these many obstacles and successfully fulfill and conquer any given assignment.

My assigned advisor surprised me at our initial meeting: he told me all the graduate beginning-level theory and performance classes would be waived. My exceptional advanced training program at Howard satisfied the Wayne State requirements. I didn't have to take any of them!

I did well in performing all my assigned roles, whether onstage or backstage, but I often found I was exhausted at the end of the day. I rarely had the time or energy to reflect on what I was learning academically. Being in the performance company was rewarding, even exciting, but I was a directing student. I needed more time for self-reflection to understand the complex theatrical process and develop an artistic vision of my own. After completing the first year, I talked over my concerns with my parents, and we came up with a new plan: I would quit the company and relinquish my graduate assistantship and living stipend, which I received for working as a company member. I would finish my degree as a regular graduate student paying full-time tuition. My parents offered to give me a monthly allowance so I could continue with this excellent academic experience without having to work to cover my living and tuition expenses.

When I met with my academic advisor, he sat in his tiny office and spoke as if he were on a throne in an academic Renaissance court. The most interesting and captivating part of his demeanor was the colorful affectations of his speech and gestures that made him sound like royalty. Most people feared him, but I was fascinated by his approach to life, his need to control everything and everyone, and his vast knowledge of theater history, which could inform one's creative choices. He was a storehouse of information as well as a delight. He agreed with my idea of leaving the company and focusing totally on fulfilling my academic requirements. He remained my advisor even after I left the company because we had established a strong academic connection and rapport.

Because I had received so many advanced placement credits and my new schedule was far more flexible, I filled it with classes in a newly formed division at the university devoted to the field of communication. The former speech program, which had morphed into an examination of the communication process and all it entails, piqued my interest. I ended up taking so many of these classes that I changed my degree in my last year from master of fine arts, which would have been appropriate for an acting, directing, or performing career, to a master of arts in theater with an added specialty in communication theory.

My academic and artistic growth flourished. This area of study, theater and communication theory, unlocked the many motivations of human behavior. It gave me an understanding of performance theory, which at that time was not part of any formal academic program of theater study. I could see, though, that exploring the performance phenomenon was the future of the performing arts. I came to think of any aesthetic form of expression as a communicative process. This understanding helped me better understand an artist's ability to reach an audience successfully. What an invaluable tool for a director to utilize in shaping an artistic vision. I had found my path.

During this last year of study at Wayne State, not wanting to depend totally on my parents for financial support, I found a part-time job. I got together with some people at Wayne State who had also left the Hilberry Company and started a traveling production of *The Fantasticks*, the musical. I agreed to direct the project and perform one of the roles. This endeavor generated some additional money, helping to lighten my parents' financial load.

The production toured all over the Detroit area and even at the summer festival in Stratford on the Avon River in Ontario, Canada. Our little production was one of the fringe productions that wasn't officially part of the festival but was offered for festival audiences nonetheless. Still, it provided the excitement of performing at one of the most acclaimed performing theater areas in the world and thus for very high-caliber, discerning audience members.

Though fun, the experience, more importantly, brought me to the attention of a producer who asked to meet with me one night after one of the performances. He talked to me about what a bright future I could have as a nightclub or professional singer. Of course, that was a hot button for me given my work in Pennsylvania after high school and my successful European tour. He convinced me that great money and connections would be possible if I signed with him as my manager. He would handle everything. Naively, I believed him and foolishly signed a contract.

At first, he arranged public performances all over the Detroit area and then booked me for private events and parties. It had become a way of generating income not just for me but for him, and, as such, he felt he could control my every movement and make my every decision.

One evening after a scheduled performance, he picked me up after the gig to drive me home. I was tired and, as such, vulnerable. Our conversation was mostly small talk at first, with a few compliments thrown in, no doubt to make me relax.

Then, it took a turn.

"Geoff, I've been thinking how wonderful it would be if you just moved in with me." My heart pounded. Even I could see such an obvious red flag.

"What?!" I asked, looking over at him. He was a middle-aged man who looked of means. He wore the best clothes, designer brands only, so I never questioned that he had money. He spoke English with no accent, but on closer look, one could tell he was from an upper-class European background. He wore a white gold pinky ring with a crest and a heavy 14-karat gold chain that draped over his chest. The more I examined his appearance, the more the word "mobster" came to mind. *I need to get out of here and this situation as soon as possible without him discovering my intentions.* He reached over from the driver's side and touched my leg.

"I could save a lot of money if you lived with me," he said. "We could get closer. I could better understand your needs, too, which means I could do a better job supporting you." I stared straight ahead at the road. I could not let him know what I was thinking. He sweetened the deal. "You wouldn't have to work as much."

Floored, I didn't know what to say. That was not what I wanted to hear. I relished my distance, my independence, my privacy. He was asking me to be his live-in partner, his significant other, or, worse, his wife or husband! At that time in my life, I could not imagine living in an intimate situation with a man in the open. I even thought that one day I might still marry, have kids, and be a more traditional family man. After all, that was what I had been taught to expect. My flirtations with men were always very well hidden.

We were in an area of the city where the streets were vacant. Detroit at that time of night became an empty desert, so I could not point to anything happening on the streets to draw his attention away from me. Fortunately, we were not very far from my apartment, so I had to endure this tension for only a small amount of time. I politely removed his hand from my leg and put it back onto his.

"Let me think about your offer," I said, "and I'll get back to you."

At first, I was insulted that he could think I would consider such a proposition. Then, I realized my trust in him, my willing familiarity, and my desire to be close had been misinterpreted. I had no desire to be intimate with this man. Nor did I want to be in such a relationship with anyone, male or female. I just wanted to be a working artist who could make a living on their talent.

Because I did not immediately respond in the affirmative, he went on.

"I've also been thinking about selling your contract to Motown Records," he said. Motown was a mover and shaker for Black performers at that time. "Think of the benefits you'd get as a Motown artist. You could work with some of the most popular Motown stars and artists. You could record with leading arrangers and songwriters. You could even become a recording star and tour for years."

At best, a Motown contract sounded like a consolation prize, offered to make me want the big deal of the day, to dangle the possibility of being kept. I wanted neither. Through the grapevine, I'd heard that if you were a Motown artist, you would be expected to do whatever its founder, Berry Gordy, said, which could be anything, including working as a backup singer or being voice-only support in a recording studio, though not always as a solo artist. In other words, the label called all the shots. Of one thing I was certain: I did not, by any means, want anyone or any organization telling me where to go, what to say, how to act, and with whom I could socialize. I wanted to be my own man. By then, I had become too confident as an artist to give my talent away as if it was nothing of great value or to let someone else determine its value.

"I'll think about Motown," I told my manager, buying myself even more time to investigate.

I immediately called my tried-and-true personal advisors, my parents, and explained what had happened. My father said he would contact a lawyer to see what wiggle room I had to break the contract. I sent him a copy of the document I had signed. His strategy worked. In no time, I was once again a free man. My parents had come to the rescue—again. I must point out, though, that this brief contractual arrangement with a manager was a great blessing in disguise because I was finally drafted. The recruitment center in Detroit called me in.

When I signed with my manager, he had me see a physician, who gave me a complete physical examination to establish a medical history. It was important that I be in good health to be able to perform at will. The doctor had asked me numerous questions, including some about my allergies and sinus problems. Throughout my childhood and as an adult, I suffered greatly from these conditions. I shared that I had been tested on several occasions and was found to be allergic to dirt, wool, and many other environmental factors. In fact, if I wore wool and it touched my skin, I would break out in a rash. The doctor wrote all this information in his report.

Troubled by what might happen next, I followed the recruitment instructions and showed up for the screening examination at the assigned time and location. I took the doctor's report in the form of a letter. All around me were men who looked like they were on their last leg. No one appeared to want to go to the senseless war in Vietnam. I watched as many young men, using all sorts of excuses, tried unsuccessfully to get sent home. I knew this was my fate, too. I knew I would be drafted.

At the end of all the testing, I successfully passed each test the physician administered during the screening. The head doctor asked that we all form one line facing him. Then he asked if anyone had any special conditions documented with papers from a physician. I raised my hand and gave him my letter. What I heard next astonished me.

"I am so sorry, son," the head doctor said. "I am going to have to eliminate you. All of the army's clothing is wool. Would you like to stay for lunch or leave now?"

"Thank you, sir," I replied, "but I think I will leave now if that is all right with you."

I flew out of there as fast as possible lest he change his mind. I left for home, knowing I had just dodged a bullet. Having avoided the draft and been released from my manager contract, I knew that my future was again bright and wide open. I could finish my studies and shape my future. I could be a professional entertainer, an actor, a director, or anything else I wished to be.

The next phone call I received was the shocker of my life. My advisor had recommended me to Wabash College in Crawfordsville, Indiana. This very small private liberal arts college had been given several million dollars to build a new theater and performing arts center. They wanted me to come to their campus, see their almost-finished facilities, and talk to them about setting up an academic theater program of study. It was a full-time job offer. The voice on the phone, that of the dean of the college, said they would fly me down to the campus and cover all my expenses.

"What do you have to lose?" he asked. "Just come and see the theater facility and tell us what you think. If you like what you see and we like you, we are prepared to offer you a faculty position." *Is this for real?* I thought. *Does this ever happen to anyone else?* And then I heard the little voice in my head saying, *The greater the risk, the greater the return.*

So I went to Crawfordsville, Indiana, to see a place and school I knew nothing about.

When my plane landed, I was met by a car and a driver. On campus, I was met by the dean, who told me a little about the history and philosophy of the college. I was then taken for a tour of the new theater facility. The school seemed to have it all together.

From the outside, the building looked like a modern brick structure—nothing very impressive. The fun began with the tour of the inside, where workers frantically ran from one place to the other. The facility was still being completed. The building consisted of a rather large lobby space with a box office, a very flexible "black box" space (a large empty performance area), huge dressing rooms for men and women, a beautiful small gallery for art exhibitions, and a main performance stage with a 500-seat house in a dramatically raked format that featured a forty-five-degree angle upward. There was also a stage house that rivaled that of a Broadway theater. The stage had lifts, trapdoors, hydraulic mechanisms, and an orchestra pit that could go up and down to form multiple configurations. Was I impressed! This space could meet any production need—except for the lighting grid over the stage. It had been built much too low, leaving little room for the fly house, the area over the stage often used for lifting scenery out of sight. The lighting grid was just above the heads of the actors, which really wouldn't work. I was surprised this design flaw had slipped through, as no performing arts designers would have approved this configuration.

When asked what I thought of the theater space, I spouted a list of changes that would have to be made to this pristine, never-used facility. The response surprised me.

"Yes, we know that changes might need to be made to the building," the dean said. "That is why we want to hire someone immediately: so changes can be implemented expeditiously. We'd like to offer you the job if you are still interested." *Oh my God, are these people for real?* They had researched me and now were prepared to bring me on board.

We talked about the contract, the salary, and the terms of this tenure-track position. All seemed to be fair, except the salary was $8,500 a year. I didn't know if one could live on so little, but those were different times, and the terms were non-negotiable.

I would be expected to teach at least one class a semester and direct two to three theatrical productions a year. *That will work*, I thought. I would also be expected to create an academic program of study that could excite the students. That sounded like fun. In addition, I'd have to help develop and design the theatrical production classes. That all sounded doable. Having just finished graduate school in theater, the whole list of duties sounded exciting and not too difficult to pull off. One more thing: I would recruit students from the general student body and advise and mentor them. What a way to put my communication skills to great use. *This could be very demanding, for not a lot of money*, I thought. Still, the excitement of being the first to work in a new building and shaping a theater program that inspired and excited students was like catnip for a theater person. I just could not resist this experience. Think of what I could learn and how I could grow artistically and personally! I had trouble hiding my enthusiasm and delight just thinking of the possibilities. I took a deep breath.

"Yes," I said. "I would be happy to accept the job." I flew back to Detroit, finished my classes for the final semester, wrote my thesis paper required for all master's degree students, graduated, and prepared myself to head back to Crawfordsville.

Wabash College, an all men's school and place of intense learning, took pride in its educational platform and the very close relationship between its faculty and students. The academic talent of the students was of the highest quality, as they were handpicked for admission. Many of the students were on some sort of scholarship or financial aid. That meant there was a great amount of diversity in the student body—a respectable number of students of color, a variety of students from wealthy to modest backgrounds, and a large number of legacy students who had a parent or other relative who'd graduated from the school. Combined, these factors made for a well-balanced first-year class each year.

The Wabash experience came at an interesting time in my life as well. I was young, energetic, and naively full of big ideas about what was possible. I possessed a great desire to explore my performance potential while preparing students for a meaningful arts experience. I found myself in charge of a multimillion-dollar performance facility and a $13,000 operating budget, quite substantial for a school its size at the time. Working with just one other faculty member whose background was dramatic literature, I was able to create—and be the first to teach—all the theater performance technique classes needed for the program.

The first day I met my colleagues—my set designer and technical director, my costume designer who was also a wonderful actress, and our secretary—and explored the many different spaces in this brand-new building was like having Christmas at the end of the summer, a most unexpected yet wonderful experience. There were no limitations on what we could do, and we tried to create the most exciting theatrical seasons possible in this new, thrilling, equipped environment. We created classical plays, farces, musicals, and theatrical classics. It was a playground of creativity and imagination.

Having never thought of becoming a teacher, I found myself often frightened by the possibility that students would ask questions I couldn't answer. There might be staging or production issues in creating the plays that I could not solve. Because it was a single-sex school, an informal environment, students would roll into the makeshift classrooms, which at times were a converted art gallery or vacant room or the theater lobby, in cutoff shorts, pajamas, a tank top, or any handy thing to cover the most minimal parts of their bodies. They would sit on the floor and be ready for a lecture I had just prepared the night before. I always had to think on my feet and be ready for whatever might occur. These were bright, demanding young men with no female distraction to divert their attention. They expected their teachers to be always on top of their game.

I had to learn not just to make up an answer for the sake of impressing the student with my knowledge but to be honest and admit when I needed to look up something and get back to the eager student who wanted an answer to their question at that very moment. I developed patience and empathy for the intellectual and emotional needs of every student, regardless of their background, acuity, or special circumstances. At times, I felt I failed to rise to the situation or meet a student's needs. But I would always reach deep inside myself and find a way to strengthen my weaknesses and my lack of knowledge and provide what each student expected or demanded of me. As I expected of them, so I expected of myself. In the end, we always grew together. I learned as I taught and grew as much as my students did.

My first class as professor of theater at Wabash College in 1970. Class was held in an art gallery while the classroom space was wrapping up construction.

Our productions were impressive, and our students became dedicated to learning as much as possible and being as creative as their imaginations would take them. This was tremendous fun, even with the long hours, which left very little time at home. Even that was okay because I was single in this small Midwestern town, and there was not much else to do. In fact, I formed a nightclub act that I performed with on the weekends at the local Holiday Inn. It kept my performing chops active while I taught daily.

Since Wabash was an all-male school, we needed women to present plays and musicals. I began aggressively recruiting females in the community who might be interested in playing some of the roles. To my surprise, there had once been a drama club in which females had played significant roles in the plays. Faculty wives and faculty children got involved. I had gotten the additional funding to correct the theater facility issues, eliminating all of my original building concerns, and I had obtained a grant from Eli Lilly to start a summer stock program that would bring professional artists to the campus and community. Another adventure was underway.

The summer stock program was to train local teachers in play production, form a support organization for them to do their productions in their local schools, and participate in and learn from all aspects of the play production process. This idea turned into a wonderful learning experience for the local teachers and an additional remuneration for me and the Wabash theater staff as we were all only on ten-month contracts. The program also provided a performance outlet for me to play the role of Cocky in the musical *The Roar of the Greasepaint—The Smell of the Crowd*. It was a most challenging yet rewarding experience for all involved.

Me in the role of Cocky in *The Roar of the Greasepaint—The Smell of the Crowd* in 1973 at Wabash College. I also produced and directed this show.

When I told my close friends that I had taken this job in Crawfordsville, many of them reminded me that this part of the country was the home of the Ku Klux Klan (KKK) and that I had better be careful. During this period in the United States, the KKK was extremely active in Indiana and was looking to establish a national presence politically. I immediately recalled the hostility I had received in the public school after desegregation and took these facts as warnings to be vigilant and aware of my surroundings and to make sure I always had a strong support system in place should I ever need to be rescued from a menacing environment. That meant I always had to be very cognizant about where I would or should not go and with whom I should or should not be seen. The college, fortunately, was always safe territory. Fortunately, the students and other faculty and staff took extra care to make sure I always felt safe and welcomed. So spending all my time on campus became my haven.

The factor I didn't consider was being the only faculty member of color and a single, young, Black, gay man living in a town where I stood out like a sore thumb. When I left the pristinely manicured lawns of the campus, I had to make sure I was never alone so as not to be physically attacked or harmed. I always checked over my shoulder. In fact, the more popular I became, the greater concern I had about my safety.

There were moments I thought I'd bitten off much more than I could chew. One such experience was when I agreed to perform in a community production of *Naughty Marietta*. I was asked to play the lead role opposite a local woman from the community. As rehearsals progressed, it seemed like any other community event, but it was not. Just before opening night, members of the cast told me that my female lead's husband was on the warpath for me because he was upset that his white wife would have to kiss a Black man onstage.

I talked to members of the company and my female co-lead. She reassured me that she would handle the situation and I had nothing to fear. Everything went off as expected, but when I met this imposing large guy after the opening night's performance, he seemed much bigger and more physically threatening than I had expected. His penetrating eye contact arrested me, but I engaged the stare anyway. I felt I should stand my ground because I was doing nothing wrong or inappropriate. His wife brought him over to meet me. I stood with great tension and concern as to what might happen next. *Would he dare hit me? Would I have to overcome a scene of struggle with this big guy, or would his wife allow him to attack me? Would I, at the very least, be embarrassed in front of my students and colleagues?* These were just some of the thoughts that rushed through my mind as I watched him approach with his wife in tow. Then, what came out of his mouth were just four words:

"You were good, too," he said and then quickly walked away.

My body, having tensed up to prepare to defend myself should this become violent, immediately relaxed. I had, once again, survived a precarious situation and was consequently stronger for having done so. I realized that I should never forget or ignore how my ethnicity could factor into my safety.

This experience of feeling vulnerable and being threatened happened more often than I care to remember. Once, I joined my students at a local bar in town after a rehearsal one evening. As I walked into the local bar, I heard, mumbled around me, derogatory racial epithets spoken just low enough for me to hear but not so loud as to make them apparent to anyone else in the bar. My students, however, must have heard or sensed what was happening because two of them grabbed my arms and quickly whisked me to a table in the opposite direction from which these comments were coming. They sat around me so no one could reach where I was seated without going through them. We never spoke of the situation or of the hatred that existed on the other side of the bar. We just laughed and enjoyed the night away as if nothing had ever happened at all. But they fully knew what they were doing and indicated through their body language that they were ready for a fight if they needed to be. This was the reality of living in a small Midwestern farm town where people hated anyone who did not look like them, particularly Black people who were educated. I realized I had to accept this situation; it reflected the racism embedded in that area of the country. I kept telling myself that the good I was doing for my students and the community—providing a positive role model of diversity—greatly outweighed the risk I was taking. More importantly, I refused to live in a state of fear.

Eventually, I found individuals and made close friends on the faculty, in the community, and on the staff who were extremely kind, giving, warm, and loving. They helped protect me at all times. I eventually realized that there were always people who had my back—defenders who genuinely cared for me and with whom I could confide and share my fears, anxieties, and dreams. I had developed close friendships.

One of the most lasting gifts of my time at Wabash was how my experiences significantly shaped my attitude and understanding of education. I learned how to be a good teacher there. Observing strong role models on the faculty, I learned to care for the students but let them go after graduation. With these colleagues, I could break bread, share my concerns, and discuss my hopes and dreams. Because of my closeness in age to the students and the long hours we often worked together onstage and offstage, I became their confidant, friend, and counselor.

My deep commitment to the students took me to some unanticipated places. For example, the local chapter of one fraternity needed an official chapter advisor for the national office. Some of the student fraternity chapter brothers arrived at my office one day with a proposal. I was sitting behind my small desk in my new faculty office. It was a modest size—no window but a place on the wall for some pictures. Since this was my first teaching job, that wall space remained blank. I thought I would eventually fill it with images of theatrical scenes I would create here at Wabash. In this spanking new, almost sanitized-looking space, I sat when two students knocked on the open door and then came in. They were curiously excited, and one said, "We have a proposal for you, but first, we have a question." This piqued my interest, but I was always afraid of what a student might ask because being a novice teacher, I didn't quite know what was too personal or appropriate. Yet I was eager to please, so I said, "Sure, what's up?"

One student continued his inquiry, "Have you ever been part of a fraternity? Ever been initiated into one?"

I said, "No. Why?"

"Because we need a chapter advisor for our fraternity, Sigma Chi, and we'd like you to be our chapter advisor. What do you think?"

"This would be great, guys," I said, "but I am not a member of your fraternity." They revealed their plan to have me enroll in enough classes at the college to qualify as a full-time student for one semester, as only fully enrolled students could be initiated. They would formally initiate me into the Delta Chi Chapter of the Sigma Chi Fraternity and then petition the national office to appoint me as their chapter advisor. The plan would first have to be approved by a three-fourths majority of all chapter members, then by the dean of the college, and finally by the national office for the fraternity. This sounded quite ambitious, but I was always up for a challenge. I had been blackballed back as an undergraduate, so this might bring some closure to that negative experience and help me understand the value of the fraternity system itself.

"If you can pull off all that," I said, "I'll do it." And they did! Everyone, including the national office, approved. In no time at all, I found myself a pledge, then going through Hell Week, and eventually installed as their chapter advisor. I started spending every free moment at the fraternity house, attending fraternity meetings, and bonding with guys I still remember fondly. I thought things couldn't get any better as a faculty member. The students in the fraternity, my classes, and on the campus respected me as their teacher, confidant, or friend. Enrollment in my classes and the theater program grew by leaps and bounds. There was never ever an abuse of the professional distance between the students and me. It was as if I was living a charmed life. My personal space was never infringed upon or compromised. I often felt like a surrogate parent; the students all loved me and treated me with respect. What a joy this became. I learned of the great value of the fraternity system and its invaluable support for students when they needed a shoulder to cry on or a brother to talk to. I helped them understand the difficulties of growing up, making choices, and depending on each other. It was and remains to this day a memory I will forever cherish.

I did find it difficult, almost heartbreaking, at my first graduation, though, when I had to say goodbye to these young men whom I'd come to care for so much. I felt as if I was being left behind, forgotten, dismissed. I had given so much of myself that I felt an enormous pain as they turned and walked away, never to look back. I concluded that, on some level, this must be what it is like when parents see their children grow up, leave the nest, and put their parents in the past as part of their history. This must be the pain of having to let go. This was the part of being a teacher I had never truly realized: letting go of your most treasured prize, your students.

Hiding (1963–1974)

While building exciting productions at Wabash College, negotiating the racial tension in Crawfordsville, and learning about teaching pedagogy, I was also offered more unusual opportunities. For example, I was asked to chaperone the Wabash College Glee Club on its European tour. Since I was so young looking, proficient at sight singing and reading music, and still possessed a strong singing voice, I was also asked to join the ensemble as one of their performers. Thinking the experience would be a hoot, I agreed, and off to Europe we went. Because this was not my first experience traveling and performing in Europe, I had little fear of being in harm's way. In fact, most audiences could not even tell I was a faculty member. Other students of color were in the glee club, so I didn't stand out as the only ethnic person singing.

The tour itinerary was uneventful for the first day or so. Then we started to have trouble with the local guides. They seemed unable to get the group anywhere on time or without a lot of effort. Because I had visited all the stops on our tour with George, I was asked to take over and steer the group from place to place. I discovered I possessed a remarkable ability to recall these earlier destinations and successfully navigate them. From that time until the end of the tour, I led the troupe all through Europe. We were never late again for a concert or an engagement for the remaining itinerary.

One night, when the entire group had turned in or gone their separate ways, I went for a walk through the local square in Florence, where people were mingling. I was off duty as a faculty member. I stood alone in the middle of the Piazza della Signoria, feeling safe in familiar territory and unencumbered by the need to protect my reputation as a faculty member. I found myself in front of the beautiful

Fountain of Neptune, a majestic, powerful display of stone and male figures surrounding a breathtaking water stream that flows into a welcoming pool. The spectacle of sight and sound drew me into its aura of romance and serenity.

Around me was Renaissance and Baroque architecture on display like in no other city in the world. The cafés and museums were just closing for the night. *How very lucky I am*, I thought, *to once again be in this spot, at this time, on such an enchanting moonlit evening.* A cool breeze passed lightly off my cheeks. *Can it get any better?*

I paused to light a cigarette, but to my surprise, my shaking hands fumbled as I reached for a lighter. I was in a foreign country where I did not speak the language, ready to relax, feeling very lonely, and couldn't even get it together to light my cigarette. At that very moment, I looked up from my awkward stance and saw a light appear in front of me. The most gorgeous dark-haired European man, about ten years older than me, was standing there, lighting my cigarette. He was the vision of a European model, with straight black hair slicked back; a defined, muscular body that showed brazenly through his clothes; and a smile that made me melt. It was like the most romantic scene ever written for a film.

He must be a hustler, I thought. He was extremely well-fashioned, after all. Some would say he was dapperly dressed. He spoke little English, but I was motivated to follow his lead. As it turned out, he was a gay medical student on break from school. We spent that night together and many more after that. When the tour went on to its next destination, he traveled with me as my guest and friend.

In Paris, where our perfect romantic storybook fling came to an end, we shared a tearful goodbye. He made it clear we'd had a temporary rendezvous and that I should not expect anything further. He went back to his life before me. Reluctantly, I returned to my conservative life as a college faculty member in Indiana, exhibiting a renewed confidence about being attractive, desired, and loved. Those memories of the affair kept my confidence of being attractive and desired alive for years.

I realized from that experience that some of life's most exciting and fulfilling moments are often fleeting and end as quickly as they begin. Never again did I take special moments for granted. They are rare gifts, precious, one-time-but-lasting experiences that make you resilient and stronger. When these times present themselves, make the most of every second—every nanosecond—and appreciate and value the entire experience to its maximum potential so there can be no thoughts of regret, just beautiful memories that last a lifetime. Time always moves on. None of us can ever go backward. Nor do I believe we should.

This European tour was one of the high points of my experiences at Wabash College even though it happened off campus. Prior to this new experience, I had been working all day and sometimes late into the night, coming home and preparing lessons for the next day. I did not believe I could find a gay personal life in Crawfordsville. I had become accustomed to living alone, being alone, and sharing some of my intimate thoughts and feelings with close friends, not with someone special. I longed for someone who would accept me for who and what I was and give me the space and support for who I was becoming.

My European lover showed me I could maintain a very satisfying private life and a public persona at the same time. I did not need to sacrifice one for the other. Learning this lesson helped me return to the Wabash campus realizing personal happiness, however fleeting, could be in the cards. I felt certain that one day, I would find the partner with whom I could share my life and build a future. Then, I would no longer have to hide but could come into the light.

I also began to understand that it was my self-confidence that attracted people to me, so I thought I would take another risk. I'd go off campus to do summer stock, a form of summer theater where plays are performed on limited budgets in a short period, generally two or three weeks, with only one- to two-week rehearsals before the production opens.

One such experience with a less-than-happy ending was my commitment to be the guest artist for a summer program dedicated to Black theater at Kalamazoo College, an elite small liberal arts college west of Ann Arbor, Michigan. I was hired to direct one show and act in another. At the onset, I thought this would be a wonderfully creative experience in a beautiful part of the country. It was anything but.

When I arrived, I was told that I would be playing the role of Lysander in Shakespeare's *A Midsummer Night's Dream*. I thought it strange that I would be cast in the part of the young lover considering I was much older than the rest of the cast and company of students. Further, I was stunned when I was informed at the dress rehearsal that I would have to wear makeup that darkened my skin so much that even I had trouble recognizing myself. Then I saw my counterpart, Helena, played by a white student in makeup so dark that it was almost shocking. When I questioned the choice, I was told by the director that his decision to use this approach was made to avoid confronting the audience with the appearance of a mixed-race couple. The artistic director of the festival hoped the audience would think I was Egyptian or the like, and the same for my partner student actress. Back then, there was no "color-blind" casting used by many theaters. For the sake of "the show must go on" and not to create a negative scene, I continued with the plan.

My time as Lysander was one of the most uncomfortable experiences I have ever had on stage. It also reinforced my belief that if I were not the director or in charge of the production, these offensive, almost abusive choices would be beyond my control. I never allowed myself to endure that kind of cultural manipulation and abuse of ethnic and racial misrepresentation again. I realized that if I were ever faced with that situation again, I would resolve these concerns well before I signed any agreements. I need to always lead with and trust in my personal beliefs, relying on my code of ethics.

That fall, I returned to Wabash to begin my fourth year. Then came my four-year pretenure evaluation; a tenure decision would be made the following year. All college and university faculty look forward to being granted tenure, an open-ended contract. Some call it being given a job for life. Tenured faculty can only be fired for just cause, which means you have done something illegal or something that otherwise greatly embarrasses the institution, such as a violation of morality. When a faculty member achieves tenure, they have academic freedom—the right to teach without censorship or institutional interference.

I was called into the dean's office—that of the same dean who had recruited me. He began by telling me what a great job I had done and was doing and recited the many accolades he had heard from the faculty, students, and the community.

"So, Geoffrey, what is next?" he said. "You must have great plans for the future. Have you thought about what they are? What are you going to do?" I was floored. My heart sank. I had done the lion's share of building this new theater program. I had helped create a major in theater and develop plans for future expansion. Yet it appeared I was being let go!

"We never thought you were going to stay here," the dean continued, "and since this is your last review before your tenure decision, I am sure you are making alternate plans."

"Are you firing me?" I asked. "I thought I was doing a good job."

"You can stay if you wish," he replied, "for one more year. I have discussed your situation with the president of the college. We agreed that we see a much bigger future for you than staying at Wabash."

He was encouraging me to spread my wings and leave this safe, comfortable, nurturing environment for greater opportunities. Leaving Wabash would be sad. I had made many close friends among the faculty and staff. The community had adopted me, so I felt close bonds with everyone, from the local dentist, whose family had become a substitute for my own, to the drummer who helped me form the little band that performed at the Holiday Inn three nights a week when I was not in a rehearsal for a play. I had assumed I would be in this little country town forever, so I had created a home there. However, whether I liked it or not, my time at Wabash was about to end.

Me in my office at Wabash College in 1974.
The poster on the wall behind me is the last show I directed at Wabash.

Fortunately, each year at Wabash, Howard University called me about teaching there. When I shared this development with my parents, my father was quick to offer advice.

"Come on home and teach at Howard," he said. "They need you. When your alma mater calls, you respond." So, once again, I followed the advice of my parents, didn't look for another position, and decided to return to Howard as a faculty member.

As the dean at Wabash had seen, I had greater things yet to achieve.

In becoming a good and caring teacher, I hoped I would pass on my mother's values to my students. Even as I grew into adulthood and developed in my career, the echoes of my parents' teachings made me aware that the choices I often made had profound consequences for me and others far into the future. By teaching, I could make a lasting impact on the lives of others. My parents believed that having respect and concern for others, particularly my students, was the best way to achieve self-respect. And achieving respect for oneself was the best way to gain self-confidence, pride in who you are, fulfillment, satisfaction, and happiness.

Often, in times of great self-doubt and uncertainty, as I grew into a successful teacher, I thought back to the fourth grade. Each time I thought of that most negative teacher in elementary school and my French teacher in high school, I resolved I would never be that type of educator. I would never be the one to discourage a student or any individual. I would always strive to become a bastion of positivity, encouragement, and motivation. I would always somehow find a way to renew my faith in myself and my students and model only positive values for all those with whom I would come in contact.

With the student body at Wabash, I was trying to find myself and develop my teaching. I felt like I was one of the guys—just a little older, perhaps, but still a very young person. I related to those students, having just been in their shoes, learning while having fun growing up. However, I still felt I was missing something: a mature perspective. I had not quite fully grown up, and I had not yet come to terms with who I really was or even what I wanted to be. Most of the time, I worked on discovering how to be a good teacher, not on how to be a happy gay Black man. I never took the time to search that side of my adult life. Discovering who I wanted to become rarely entered my mind. I spent all my time focusing on what I needed to accomplish each day. I kept myself distracted by always doing rather than thinking about how one day built on another or about long-term goals. And because I was so close to my students' age and fresh out of graduate school, I found it easier to identify more with them than with my faculty colleagues.

Maybe the Wabash dean was right: I needed to spread my wings, leave my comfort zone, and learn to fly alone. But could I really do that in the same town where my father lived and in the same place my father worked? It felt like I might just be following the path of least resistance and doing what my parents wanted me to do. However, it wasn't as if my parents had ever given me poor advice. I have always benefited from their guidance. Yet this deep-seated feeling of not pursuing my own choices and not finding my path weighed heavily on my mind. How could I live on my own terms if I had to play yet another role, the son of a prominent figure on a big university campus? Even at age twenty-six, I had not yet entirely grown up. *Would I always have to live in the shadow of my father? Would I always feel I had failed when I saw my peers in the movies, onstage, on television?* These were my burning thoughts.

Yet returning to Howard University could promote another type of growth. There, I could grow as a professor. I gained immense knowledge, joy, and excitement through the educational enterprise at Wabash: exploring new ways of life, finding innovative approaches to problem-solving, gaining and sharing a limitless eagerness and excitement for living life itself. The more I learned, however, the more I realized what I did not know. The more I grew personally and artistically, the more new bodies of information I could share with my students. Yes, I learned what it was like to be a good teacher at Wabash, but my growth still felt partial.

I therefore put aside any hesitations, reservations, and fears I had and accepted the position Howard University offered me. I concluded that I was not really going backward; I was moving forward in a more familiar environment. The Wabash College dean had said as much. I felt I could grow immensely from taking this step and better learning how to address the needs of Black students. I would learn more about Black cultures from around the world and, in doing so, more about myself as a Black man. I trusted that broadening my perspective would also expand my understanding of how I, a gay Black man, could fit into this complicated and sometimes perplexing world of which I was just a small part.

I was entering a precarious situation at Howard. The students had maintained the dissident, adversarial relationship with the faculty that had been forged during the sixties protest movement. Civil rights issues were still prominent for these politically aware young Black students, and the faculty found it difficult to balance student demands with academic rigor.

In my welcoming interview, the dean of the College of Fine Arts shared that she felt the drama department needed to teach, once again, good theater techniques and skills, foster an appreciation for classical training, and help students master traditional theater in addition to Black theater. I faced a great challenge because my assignments were teaching acting skills and period acting techniques, the very topics the students found irrelevant because of their connection to traditional white theater.

As I walked around Howard to meet the faculty and students, I was shocked at how the facilities had been neglected. The beautiful old campus appeared to be falling apart. The classically designed Ira Aldridge Theater, once the pride of the university, reminded me of a broken-down car left unmaintained and rusting in a yard. Over the years, the students had worn the buildings down to their bones. Maintenance had been deferred so much that it seemed like millions of dollars would be needed to restore the campus to its glory days, not to mention the money required to expand the facility to accommodate increased enrollment, which was the department's goal—quite a change from the magnificent building at Wabash.

At that time, the College of Fine Arts was a low priority for an investment of university resources. It was not even certain the university would continue to support the college as a stand-alone unit. As I walked through the hallways lined with marquee-size posters advertising past theatrical productions, I remembered my student years, when I wondered whether my name would ever be proudly displayed on these walls. An excitement built inside me as I remembered those days of high hopes and big dreams. Bubbling right alongside my excitement was the reality of how difficult this job would be. If I stayed, I would need to help change these shocking conditions.

To be successful, I had to teach and help acquire desperately needed resources and facilities. I would need to seek university support to build new programs of study rather than having support freely offered, as it had been at Wabash. I would have to acquire new funding to continue the once-impressive play production program.

I wondered if I had made the right decision. I had come from a school where money and resources were plentiful and where my ability to rally support and resources for the arts could make all the difference for student success. At that moment, I realized that maybe, just maybe, Howard was handing me an opportunity to apply what I had learned at that exclusive school to students who truly needed me. I could make a difference. That missing piece inside me—finding purpose and meaning for my work and understanding what I could do—became clearer. This position could be the beginning of a change for the better, not just for the department and the college but for me. I wasn't trying to return to my youth or "the good old days." I could start here and go forward.

The other faculty members seemed to be a hodgepodge of individuals led by a chairman whose demeanor was right off the mean streets. He spoke in a Black, pseudo-hip vernacular with a bully attitude that rivaled my brother's. He saw himself as the one in control and, as he used to say, "It's my way or the highway." His misogynistic treatment of the female faculty and domineering attitude toward everyone else proclaimed his need to control each teacher's professional as well as personal life. Ultimately, this became his downfall.

Many might have wondered if he even had a college degree and, if so, how he ever got it. Yet he was chairman of the drama department. *I've seen this before with my brother*, I thought. *I just need to deal with him like a bully: stand my ground for what I believe in and don't back down.* I would learn later from the faculty who openly welcomed me to the university that as I was approaching the building for the first time to meet the dean, this fellow was meeting with some of his most trusted faculty supporters. As the story goes, he looked out the window and, noticing my approach, turned to those assembled and said, "This guy thinks he is going to be my replacement, and I will not sit by and allow that to happen. I will fight him tooth and nail." Every chance he got, he tried to do just that.

Our battle began when he gave me my first assignment to direct Langston Hughes's *Tambourines to Glory*, a rarely performed musical. Having staged many musicals at Wabash, however, I was very comfortable directing and producing this form of theater. The department chair made this assignment more of a test of what I could do, though. He crippled the show with a small budget and little advertising. And because there was no musical theater program at that time, I was also required to find students who could sing, dance, and act. I spent untold hours thinking about how to find student actors. I held numerous auditions, worked with the faculty designers to create low-budget sets and costumes for the play, and coordinated with a musical director who taught the actors the music and directed the band.

Fortunately, one of the training techniques I learned in undergraduate and graduate school was how to produce and direct theater with little to no resources. The students, of course, were oblivious to the funding issues and the test set for me by the chairman. Their expectations soared. Going back to fight the chairman for more money seemed a waste of time. I knew that if I were to succeed, I would have to find a way to make up for what I lacked in financial support. I needed to tell this story without impressive sets and costumes. Eventually, I realized that all I really needed were actors who understood and could relate to the power of gospel music given that the story was set in a Black church environment. I visualized that I could focus on the performances of these student actors and devised a plan to make the production about the characters' faith using traditional gospel songs. I'd let their passion carry the story to the audience. After all, gospel music can penetrate the soul of its listeners. I reinterpreted the play to support this approach and selected powerful, moving gospel songs widely known in the Black church community to help the audience feel at home.

I cast one of the better singers and actresses in the student body. She had a gospel voice that gave you chills as her sound touched your heart. Given that the text and 1950s music were so dated, I wanted to create a meaningful moment for the ending. I staged her starting the last song, singing on stage—a quiet hum that built into the powerful song "Amazing Grace." I had her finish the song as she slowly walked through the audience to the exit. As she walked defiantly off the stage, the curtain slowly closed behind her, and the houselights brightened to indicate the end of the play. There was a moment of silence before the audience burst into a standing ovation.

The cast, featuring Marva Hicks, performing *Tambourines to Glory* at Howard University.

The student newspaper, the *Hilltop*, called the production spectacular. Yet the department chairman somehow could not acknowledge me with anything remotely close to "congratulations" or "good job." He claimed I had used theatrical tricks. What he called tricks I called techniques.

Techniques are what I taught: "Techniques of Acting," "Acting Styles," and "Period Styles of Acting." And I was very good at teaching acting, though I'd often be so drained after class that I'd be ready to collapse.

My production of *Tambourines to Glory* sold out, and my star student, Marva Hicks, went on, after graduation, to become a very successful Broadway performer and recording artist. Many years later, I saw her perform with Lena Horne in *The Lady and Her Music*. What an excitement it was to meet Ms. Horne backstage and hear her rave about Marva's talent and outstanding professional training. As was true with many of my students, her successful career became my greatest reward. Teaching really was my calling—helping students recognize their potential, discover how to use their many talents, and develop their self-confidence so that they trusted and believed in themselves as artists and caring human beings. I pinpointed my professional purpose: inspiring and facilitating others in sharing their talent to their maximum potential. That was why I had come to Howard: to release the energy of others so that they could share their talent with the world.

Because *Tambourines to Glory* evidenced my strong knowledge of theater and acting, the chairman never again put obstacles in my path or criticized my approach to teaching or directing. I had learned that the audience's thunderous applause was the real feedback I needed to assess the actors' effectiveness on the stage, regardless of what critics within or outside the institution might think or say. At that point, I was establishing my career as an educator and garnering the respect of my colleagues in the field, but I still had some work to do. I knew I'd won a battle but still needed to win the war. I needed to gain greater respect and trust from more of the faculty and even greater buy-in from the students.

My next accomplishment required a steep learning curve. I had come from teaching at Wabash, a small private all-male liberal arts college where less than eight percent of the student body represented historically marginalized groups. I landed at Howard, a prestigious midsize publicly funded yet privately run university where less than one percent of all students and faculty were white. The faculty reflected the same ethnic makeup or numbers as the student body. Yet the faculty and students were extremely diverse in their backgrounds and points of view. At commencement, the academic regalia displayed bright colors, patterns, and fabrics from many African regions and tribes from more than twenty countries. This collage—a spectacle of colors, shapes, and traditional dress, robes, drapes, and internationally representative textiles and fabrics—became an interesting and sometimes amazing blend of visual delights, but it was always extremely enlightening and illustrative of the multifaceted world in which we live. For me, personally and professionally, each time I experienced this fashion display, I learned more about the vast differences and similarities of the world's differing cultures.

Over time, I learned that the fine arts faculty and students came from all walks of life. Some were from highly respected educational backgrounds, others from successful careers in the industry. Another segment comprised exceptionally gifted performing and studio artists who saw Howard University as a refuge from the colder, unwelcoming white society. There were also others like the department chair, who, as the dean of the College of Fine Arts once told me, "was one of the only faculty who could handle the often angry and frustrated students of the times in which we lived."

Eventually, I was asked to head the acting and directing programs and direct at least one production a year. The schedule and workload seemed much lighter than I'd become accustomed to at Wabash College. Rather than directing three productions, I had only one. And rather than teaching three to four classes a semester, I had only two to three teaching assignments a term. The schedule never proved to be a problem. However, the drama of the people who surrounded me filled much of my time. The drama department always provided excitement, debate, strong differences of opinions, and diverse points of view. I was always challenged to be my best.

I willingly entered the fight to shape the department's philosophy, which would guide its future. I constantly delineated and defended my vision, saying that the students and I could reach extraordinary heights of exceptional artistic expression; grow as individual artists, scholars, and global citizens; and possess a unique voice that clearly communicated the innermost thoughts and feelings of a human being. Many shouting matches and heated pedagogical debates, both inside and outside the classroom, ensued almost every day.

These ongoing discussions, debates, and even arguments made me constantly re-center my most sacred beliefs about education, society, and the world in which we live. What emerged in me was a greater mission as a teacher, guide, friend, and colleague, and my greatest period of personal and professional growth occurred. I helped shape a program of study that prepared Black performers to be successful in a primarily white industry—to be artists who had to be reckoned with, accepted on their terms, valued, and at times even revered.

At that point in Howard's evolution, the students resented and mistrusted traditional study in the arts, calling it "white education."

Hiding (1963–1974)

They fought and argued with any teacher who thought otherwise, and that included me. I spent my first year trying to understand two points of view: that of the students and that of the few faculty who seemed to enjoy agitating the students. *How could I reach either of them?* Faculty meetings became intense debates regarding the training program and correct pedagogy.

Many times, the drama in the department was exposed in the hallways, the student and faculty lounges, and even faculty meetings. Faculty would yell and scream at each other, losing their tempers in the middle of meetings. On one occasion, a playwriting professor leaned into me and said loudly, "You better watch your back when you leave here because I'm gonna get you, man, when you least expect it."

"Bring it on," I said. "You can't intimidate me." Heightened emotions accompanied extraordinary talent. And exceptional talent was always a part of the Howard experience and had been since its founding in 1867.

My experience growing up with a bully brother became unusually helpful in handling this and other situations in which I needed to stand my ground.

Howard was the mecca for educating Black students from all over the world. Studying the arts there carried a reputation: students were thought to be in touch with the pulse of Black culture. I felt called to help students see how they might navigate both the white and Black arts cultures. My pedagogical successes moved faculty and students toward the understanding that acquiring professional theatrical techniques was not "acting white." Black theater technique could trace its roots to the history of theater even as it expressed its view of life. It was not going to be easy convincing the students to believe in this approach and make the changes I envisioned. But I had to make every effort.

BETTER TO CRY NOW

The days of students at the knees of a faculty member were over, as screaming matches between students and faculty attested. Students openly, loudly demanded what they thought they needed and wanted. They rejected any direction from anyone. The scene was a far cry from what I was used to experiencing in the classroom. Students verbally fought the faculty for a grade, even a plus or minus. These were tough times, not so terribly unlike my student days at Howard, with one big difference: I was a faculty member trying to convince and teach the students rather than one of the outspoken, often disruptive students.

My challenge was changing students' attitudes from argumentative, angry, and negative to creative, self-challenging, and positive. How? By focusing on technique and growth. My communication background, confidence, and youthful appearance gave me an advantage. I was a new face with new ideas, so the students were inclined to listen to me, but I still had to gain their trust. So I listened to their needs, spoke to them as stakeholders in the changes underway, and constantly remained an advocate for improvement and growth. As they grew and matured, I did, too. I gained new insights into my creative process and heightened and refined my communication skills.

At one point, I developed a following of first-year students. Each had been a star in their high school or church. So they all thought they were the cat's meow. They looked to me as their parental leader, from whom they should only get encouragement, praise, and adoration. They seldom wanted to hear harsh criticism, but at times, that's exactly what they needed to hear.

Initially, I gave them the positive feedback they craved but then realized it would do them little to no good when they were on the stage and I was not. Then, they'd have only one thing to rely on: their craft. One day after class, I gathered them in my office. There were maybe ten students crammed into this very small space. Some students had to sit on the floor, lean against the walls, or stand. They filled every available space. It was so tight, I could almost hear and feel them breathing, consuming what little air was available.

Having just completed a rigorous acting class, they were all tired, vulnerable, and ready to listen so they could make their exit as quickly as possible. At first, I was hesitant but passionately felt that I had to push them into a deeper understanding of why they had to improve their performance technique. I began my remarks:

> "I have to share a most important point with you. From this time forward, I will no longer tell you only what is working in your acting performance. I am also going to share, without softening the blow, the mistakes that I believe you are making and challenge you to self-correct those mistakes. Class time is too valuable to spend so much time on individual critiques.
>
> "You must learn to observe each other more intensely, too, and learn from each other as much as you learn from me and my feedback. Soon, there will come the day when you and your acting technique must stand alone. To be ready for that day, you must be able to take and process feedback from me and your peers.
>
> "You also need to learn from all your experiences, wherever they happen. You must be able to learn and grow from any professional performances you encounter, from other actors like yourselves, and from what you see on any stage, television, or film."

I looked around the room. They were all listening.

"You must be learning all the time, not just when you get a critique regarding a particular monologue or scene. If you don't, you will have to accept you'll be no better than mediocre. You will be stuck at the same level of performance technique.

"To improve, you also must find *your* path by relying solely on *your* wits, by trusting *your* instincts. In the professional world, there's always someone else ready and able to do your job, so you must anticipate when you are going down the wrong path with a role or character. And you must have the courage to try a new approach that works better.

"Most importantly, you cannot wait until you graduate to start this behavior. You have to start functioning this way right now. Develop your sensibilities *now*. Find an acting approach that works for you *now* so you can develop fast enough to keep pace with the demands of a production or an opportunity. Question everything you do in every performance, and discover ways you can do it better. Do this over and over and over until there are no other avenues to explore."

As expected, some students heard my message. Heads nodded in the affirmative. Some, however, did not seem to have a clue as to what I'd just said. They just stood, silently waiting until it was time to leave. Others asked questions to get greater clarity. Another group only needed time to process my words into action.

These were all reactions I had anticipated. You win some and always lose some. These are the consequences every teacher experiences.

Overall, though, I learned that the harder I pushed my students to demand more of themselves than was asked, the better they became as artists who could recognize the differences between being good, great, and exceptional. This approach helped me and them better understand the communicative process every actor goes through to achieve complete believability onstage. In fact, it became the subject of my doctoral dissertation in communication theory.

Me in 1980, right after being appointed chair of the drama department at Howard University.

I studiously solicited support from my colleagues, too, by listening to their ideas, fostering a team approach that made space for each artist's vision, and building new programs of study in nontraditional environments. I encouraged students and faculty to participate in regional theaters or with other performing organizations. I also modeled this behavior personally by directing at Montgomery College and George Washington University. I helped build performing arts organizations in the local community neighborhoods and centers.

I entered the students and their productions in nationally competitive organizations, such as the American College Theater Festival. After a time, the students started winning acting awards, recognition, and praise for their expertise and outstanding talent.

Eventually, we established a reputation for high-quality professional training and performance rigor, which instilled pride in Howard's performing arts students and faculty. We sought and received national accreditation for our performing arts programs. I even received the American College Theater Festival Award of Excellence from the John F. Kennedy Center for the Performing Arts, given to only one recipient each year in each region of the United States.

And it all started with a frank conversation.

When I was at Howard University, the faculty would socialize in and out of the workplace. There was always a buzz around the classrooms and hallways, in the workspaces and studios. New thoughts and ideas were being germinated in the most unusual circumstances and places. It was common to go to someone's house in the evening for wine and cheese or attend social events in town with other colleagues.

During this period, I went to a cocktail party at a faculty member's home and got into a discussion with my colleague, Sandra Bowie, about issues of gender and equity. Her feeling was that a man could not possibly understand and be sensitive to female issues. I vowed to write a musical revue expressing a female point of view regarding gender issues of equality for women. I went even further, getting her to promise to perform the piece for an audience if she found I had succeeded.

Hiding (1963–1974)

Me in 1977, enjoying an evening with Howard University colleagues.

I created *Reflections of a Woman*, based on the poetry of Gwendolyn Brooks and the music of Melissa Manchester. In poetry and song, this musical montage presented a female perspective that expressed the fears, anxieties, frustrations, anger, and love that a woman experiences daily. Another faculty colleague agreed to design and build the set, and yet another agreed to produce the revue. In the end, it turned out to be an expressive and convincing cavalcade of feelings set to music. The production touched every audience for whom it was performed. Sandra was brilliant. She showed the students how an actress—she won the Helen Hayes Award for Best Actress in a Musical or Play—could also win the hearts of any audience. Even though the play was not staged in a professional regional theater, it provided a role model of the best in acting and performance for the Howard students.

We toured *Reflections of a Woman* in high schools and small community centers, where audiences consistently responded with thunderous applause. The production forged a lasting relationship with Sandra, who remains a trusted friend to this day.

Sandra Bowie in 2005, on the evening of the opening of the Alexander Kasser Theater. We've been friends for years, challenging each other and growing together along the way. She provided me with the inspiration to create *Reflections of a Woman* in 1980, in which she delivered an outstanding performance in the starring role.

We would all come to say, "If you can make it at Howard, you can make it anywhere." My days at Howard, starting as a student through my thirteen years as a faculty member—four as chairman of the drama department—taught me something vital: one can find strength in adversity, learn from conflict, and rise above and beyond obstacles on the pathway to achieving one's goals.

I was at my professional peak. I grew personally as my skills as an artist developed. I discovered a way to speak my truth through my art, found my voice as a person of color, and continued to grow as a teacher. This period of my life was a creative potpourri in building confidence artistically and personally. I realized that I could be both an artist and a teacher. I could let go of the perception that teaching was a consolation prize for people who could not make it professionally. The feeling that I had failed to achieve each time I saw artists with whom I had gone to school performing successfully onstage or on television or film began to pass. I started to recognize that my success as a teacher was how I could change the lives of young developing artists, making my mark on the world. Those students who accepted my coaching, built upon my teachings or lessons, and used those newfound tools to be better artists, communicators, or vehicles of change became, for me, an even greater success than my being a performer. I could provide my students with the ability to transform audiences through their art, to make a lasting impact on those who heard their voice and understood their message. This became my greater goal and provided enormous happiness and fulfillment. It became my calling.

I still seemed to lack that strength and direction that comes from finding another individual with whom you can bond, become one, and make you feel you are not alone when making your way through the world. However, I trusted in the belief that love comes when you least expect it. Just keep your eyes open and your heart ready to share when that moment occurs. For now, I decided to focus on my work and goal of becoming the best educator who uses their gifts to inspire others.

ACT 3

EMERGING (1975-1987)

IN THE MIDSEVENTIES, I was twenty-eight and teaching in the Howard University drama department. As I was carousing one evening at an establishment in Georgetown, I reconnected with a buddy. I'll call him Brandon, a classmate from my undergraduate years at Howard. He would later become a successful professional performer. But back then, he was a very popular local folk music performer in DC, living above one of the hottest nightclubs in Georgetown, the Cellar Door. He befriended many celebrities and, by his own account, was one himself.

Brandon and I regularly took off the weekend, got in my little blue MGB (a two-door British racing sports car), and drove to the beach for another party. One evening, after returning from such a trip, Brandon called. He said he had a good feeling about that night. "Let's go out for a drink," he said. Usually, that meant a trip to the DC Eagle, a gay nightclub, one of our favorite stomping grounds. I agreed, and off we went.

We were standing at one of the more popular walkways in the bar when a striking young man walked past us. We both noticed what a hot-looking guy he was. He even smiled as he passed. Brandon and I had developed a little game we played in the bars: if one of us saw someone of interest, the other would be deployed to meet him, bring him back to our circle, and introduce him to the one waiting for the encounter. This system helped eliminate the feeling of rejection if the person was not interested in a connection. It put no one at great risk.

In that instance, it was Brandon who was interested in this attractive stranger, so I was deployed to meet him and, as planned, play my role. I turned, facing this hunky, athletic-looking blond guy, and introduced myself. He said his name was Ed, and he was from Syracuse, New York. He had just finished college and recently moved to DC.

"Let me introduce you to my friend, Brandon," I said. "Come on with me."

Ed Snyder, my partner and husband, in 2005, when he had the great opportunity to live in Basel, Switzerland, for a few years. Look at that smile—of course it captured my heart.

When we arrived where Brandon was standing, I completed my task and stepped aside. They talked a bit, but Ed seemed more interested in me than my friend. As I continued to move away from them, allowing Brandon and Ed space to talk, Ed kept moving even closer to me. I eventually got the message: I was Ed's target, not my friend or anyone else. A spark of electricity seemed to arc between us.

Ed and I fell madly and passionately in love. By the end of the evening, Brandon had disappeared, and we had become a couple. By the end of the week, we were living together. Ed gave me a foundation of unconditional love, support, and encouragement that had been lacking in my life. Once we connected emotionally, physically, and spiritually, I felt complete. I believed that with him by my side, no hurdle was too high to overcome. We could both face life openly as a gay couple. These were times, however, when being openly gay was not always acceptable. So many times, we were labeled as best friends, roommates, and "extremely close." In the gay community, though, we were a couple.

At first, it was not easy for us to find careers we could pursue without compromising one or the other. But whenever either of us had professional doubts or a personal crisis, we turned to the other for support and strength. Challenges surfaced, including jobs that demanded we be apart for weeks, months, or even years. By relying on our love for each other, we conquered great distances, overcame external forces that threatened to pull us apart, and always reaffirmed that we were stronger together than apart. In addition, we found we could achieve independence as well as unity while pursuing separate opportunities yet still always remain close as one happy, content, united couple. That strength enabled each of us to take huge risks in building each of our careers.

This became the classic love story. We rode bicycles along the Georgetown Canal, had picnics in Rock Creek Park, went to parties and the discos together, and could and would spend the entire day and night just talking and enjoying each other's company. We had breakfast, lunch, and dinner together just about every night. Within our first week of meeting came Ed's birthday. I decided to throw a party for him with the few people who knew we had become a couple. At that time, I had an apartment in the Twin Towers, a new high-rise in downtown Silver Spring, just across the DC border. I had not discussed any of these plans with him but asked him to meet me at my place. He showed up, and our group of friends all shouted, "Surprise!" as I opened the door to greet him. He was stunned, but I wanted to show him how much I cared. It turned out to be a great evening of fun for everyone, including Ed. At one point during the evening, I pulled Ed aside and took him into a vacant room in the apartment. I told him I had a birthday gift I wanted to share.

He followed me, and I said, "I want to give you a present, one that means very much to me."

I had purchased a gold chain identical to the one I was wearing. I said, "This chain I am wearing is one of the most valuable and important items in my possession. It has been with me through my many ups and downs. It is the most important thing I own, and I consider it my good luck charm."

I took it off my neck and put it around his and then revealed the matching chain I had just purchased and put it on my neck and said, "Now, as we wear these perfectly matched chains, I want both of us always to remember that we will always be connected and shine together for all to see, just like these bright gold chains glimmer in the light. So will we. You see, we are now one."

We never saw ourselves in competition with each other. We always

Emerging (1975–1987)

saw ourselves as a couple experiencing and celebrating our individual careers together. We saw our individual achievements as mutual and joint successes and our challenges as shared goals. We showed each other avenues that we could not have seen separately. We each decided that, whenever possible, we would live openly as a gay couple and eventually go from civil union to marriage. (Gay marriage was illegal in Washington, DC, and New Jersey for most of the time we lived there. Legalized civil union was eventually granted for gay couples, and by the time we moved to California, gay marriage had been officially legalized in both states.) We did just that. We actually married twice as we moved from one state, New Jersey, to another, California, because of the laws changing at different times in each state.

When we introduced ourselves to our respective families, both tribes embraced us. On one occasion, when I went home to see my parents without Ed, they asked, "Where's Ed?"

"He feels that whenever I come home, he doesn't always have to accompany me," I explained. "He doesn't want to feel that he is intruding on my time with you."

"Let me call him," my father said. He dialed and addressed Ed directly. "You are a part of this family. Whenever we see Geoffrey, we expect to see you, too."

I knew then that my parents felt the same love for him as they felt for me. Similarly, when Ed's mother was terminally ill and had reached her last hours, I called to see how Ed was holding up and how she was doing. She asked to speak to me.

"Take care of my Eddie," she said. Those were some of her last words spoken before she passed.

As we grew from our twenties into our thirties, forties, fifties, and older, we continued to learn from each other and grow from our mutual wisdom. We came of age together, and yes, we had our struggles, as is typical with most couples. We fought off and silenced those who wanted to see if they could break us up. We explored our career goals together, even when that meant we would not physically be together for one year or more. And we always talked and communicated with each other every day, regardless of the distance between us. We never went to sleep angry or frustrated with each other. We always tried to reassure each other that regardless of the issue or problem, we could find a solution by working through it together.

That empty place once inside me was now full of love. We found that, with great love and respect, you can climb the highest of mountains and overcome the greatest obstacles. You see, we became soulmates. We were also social climbers in the gay community. At least we tried to be.

Ed and I rented a beautiful new townhouse in the Adams Morgan neighborhood of Washington, DC, filled with lovely old Washingtonian townhouses built in the late 1920s and 1930s. They were grand buildings with multiple floors, three or even four stories, Victorian styled with remarkable features, such as ornate marble stone fireplaces that actually functioned.

The leading interior designer in the city, an icon on the gay circuit, owned one such home. People fought for an invitation to his parties; one of those was considered a ticket that proved you'd made it into the upper echelon of affluent gay society. The interior designer's house was on the same block as ours. We did not know this designer very well, but we badly wanted to attend one of his elaborate affairs. There was no use trying to waltz in; bouncers at the door checked a very detailed list to see whether you'd been invited.

At the time, Ed and I shared our townhouse with a disco-scene-dancer boy who was invited to all the high-fashion parties in DC. He made it a point to be seen at all the right parties with all the right people. The interior designer's invitation list included some of the hottest, most attractive, and most connected people in the city who would come, pose, and model, hoping to be photographed for the *Advocate* or some other posh gay magazine.

Our roommate, George, came home one night from the disco and announced that the top decorator was having a party across the street and that he had managed to get us all invitations. If we played our cards right, he said, attending the soiree could put us on the A-list for gay Washington. This party was one of the finest and most glamorous events of the year. Ecstatic, we bought fashionable outfits, had our nails and hair done to look our best, and arrived at the party fashionably late so as not to appear too eager.

The biggest bodybuilder I had ever seen, one gorgeous man, greeted us at the door.

"Your name?" he asked. His voice was deep.

We gave him our names, and to my surprise, he found them far down on the long list he so proudly protected.

The house looked like a Hollywood high-end, over-budget movie set. Stunning male servers carried trays with drinks and food platters that made you think you were at the White House. Everything was simply elegant. After an hour, I started to feel tired, even a little faint. My shoes hurt, too, even though fashion knows no pain.

Nevertheless, it had been a long day. I glanced at a beautiful small chair in the corner of the room. Ever so gracefully, I moved toward the chair, stood in front of it, and slowly began to sit. The room was so crowded that I was unable to really look at this piece of furniture. All I needed was a sturdy chair where I could sit for a couple of minutes and then stand back up and rejoin the party. No one was paying any attention to me anyway.

As I sat in the chair, it completely gave way, landing on the floor with a huge crashing sound that stopped everyone in the room. All heads immediately turned to see what I had done. The music stopped. All conversation stopped. Our host suddenly appeared.

"That was a priceless seventeenth-century chair," he said. "Leave immediately."

A pathway cleared in front of me as, in total silence, the hunky bouncer helped lift me off the floor. He then escorted me back to the door. Ed followed. Every eye was on me as I had become the outcast they would all remember. The looks were attacking, mean, hostile. No one asked if I was all right or injured. No one seemed to care about anything but the old chair. I could not leave fast enough for anyone.

Needless to say, we were never invited back to any A-list party. Instead, I became the story that people would share about the lower-class person who did not know how to behave. Life went on, though, and we did find true friendship that same year.

During my time at Howard, a gay couple from the music department offered both Ed and me subtle guidance we didn't appreciate enough at the time. They were charming, talented, gracious people, LeRoy Dorsey and Clyde Parker. At the time, they were the only gay couple we'd ever met who had been together for more than thirty years. They called us their "boys" and showed us that a loving, long-lasting relationship was possible in the gay community.

LeRoy and Clyde provided a family setting for discussing personal and political issues and LGBTQ+ local and national concerns. They gave us advice about managing a gay commitment in a straight world. We could ask them anything and get a straightforward, loving answer that always steered us in the right direction. They would often say, for instance, how we mustn't prejudge people by how they looked, spoke, or acted. At that time, the gay community was obsessed with masculinity and being "butch." Gays themselves often looked down upon or ridiculed gay folks with "affectations," feminine gestures, or attitudes. The ideal was to be as masculine as possible so the straight community could not possibly call you names, label you as obviously gay, or use words such as "faggot" or "queer" in hateful manners. It was a time of keeping up appearances.

LeRoy and Clyde taught us to accept all gay people, whether butch, feminine, or bisexual, and see past language used to hurt others and attitudes that exclude them. They taught us the power of loving acceptance of all and being able to walk in someone else's shoes. How important that lesson became for Ed and me throughout our life as a couple.

Clyde, a talented pianist, was also an outstanding cook who served up the best and most tantalizing Southern-style, scrumptious meals. Everyone assembled near his kitchen would enjoy watching him cook as he talked and laughed about all kinds of subjects. He never lost sight of the meal preparation, though he would get animatedly involved in each lively debate.

The other half of the couple, LeRoy, the head of voice in the Howard University music department, had Jessye Norman as his star pupil. He had such a booming baritone–bass voice that when he spoke, the words that came out of his mouth sounded like a declaration from God himself. Having been a professional opera singer, he carried himself with all the trappings of a great diva. LeRoy was a big man, well over six feet tall, and yet he was so very loving and tender. He warmed our hearts each time we were in his presence. He was just one big sweetheart. He and Clyde treated Ed and me as if we were two of their children.

They taught us how to overcome the negative external pressures that the larger society often shows to gay people and couples and how to conform to traditional values and behaviors without compromising beliefs or principles. They helped us face and confront individuals who wished to define our lives in terms other than those we chose. We learned that the solution was to discuss whatever issue arose around us or tried to come between us, however hard these conversations appeared to be or how sensitive they were to discuss.

Clyde and LeRoy told us of events we needed to experience and introduced us to gay and straight people in the arts and education who, in their judgment, we should know. They even adopted and raised a straight Hispanic young man who always treated them as loving parents. They were very special, and everyone in their circle of friends knew how lucky they were to know them. Their close friends included noteworthy musicians such as Leontyne Price; they would party with her when she was in the area or travel to catch one of her performances.

This great couple treated us as if we were their closest family members and continued to provide us with a home away from home, a safe place where we could always be relaxed and loved. They held elaborate weekly parties and social gatherings with interesting people, sometimes leaders from the community. Some were gay. Some were straight. All enjoyed witty dialogue and intellectual discussions. Going to their home, which we did often, was a treat because we never knew who would be on the guest list or what tantalizing gossip they had recently heard. Ed and I felt honored to be in their circle of friends and part of their family. They helped us believe that we, too, could last forever together as a couple.

One day in 1979, I was sitting in my office on the Howard campus when I got a telephone call from an unknown overseas number. The person on the other end sounded official and spoke English with

Emerging (1975–1987)

a German accent. He said he and the Stadttheater in St. Gallen, Switzerland, were interested in producing the European premiere of *Raisin*, the musical.

"We are planning to cast the leads out of New York City but were wondering if you could cast the remaining performing company and select the rhythm section of the orchestra from Howard University students and faculty," he explained.

And that wasn't all. They wanted me to prepare the players, serve as associate director, come to Europe, rehearse the production, and tour the musical throughout Switzerland and Germany. Was I interested?

Yes, absolutely! My heart was beating a mile a minute as my mind raced. *Can I do this? Absolutely, yes!* I was more than interested, so I continued to respond in the affirmative. The gentleman said that was what he wanted to hear and that he and the theater would work out the details and get back to me.

Of course, if the experience came to pass, performing in Europe would not seem like a great stretch because I had done it successfully twice before: with George as a singing duo and with the Wabash College Glee Club. The job would include huge additional responsibilities, but the challenge already had engaged my mind, heart, and soul. What an incredible opportunity this could be for me, the faculty, and my students.

That phone call launched an international project that took the next year to come to fruition and the following year to execute, with lots of high points and surprises along the way.

During the planning phase, the projected cost became a moving target in part because of the continued fluctuation of the US dollar. The Swiss theater sponsoring the project anticipated their costs would rise by more than twenty to thirty percent in two to three months. Then came the next shocking telephone call: the total project cost had increased so significantly that the project cost in American dollars had reached the point where they needed to cancel. What was once financially doable had become unmanageable.

In my mind, canceling the project would bypass one of the most unique experiences the faculty, students, and I had ever planned, so I would not give up easily. I bought some time by saying I would explore whether the university could pick up some of the costs for its faculty and students. Immediately, I went to the dean of the college to see if my suggestion was possible. As I suspected, the university said they had no money to cover these unusual expenses, and I should just, as suggested, cancel the project. This turn of fate was still unacceptable. I had to find a way to raise money or otherwise cover the rising expenses.

I came up with another idea: I would build another production that focused on the evolution of American Black music from African rhythms to the doo-wop R&B sounds of the 1950s and 1960s. I believed this additional production, to be performed by the students in the *Raisin* ensemble, would provide the revenue needed to underwrite the rising costs of the *Raisin* tour. It would also provide a way to share Black music with a European audience. Production costs would be minimized by using costumes from the existing university inventory. Also, students would do the choreography, and I would direct.

I found a little-known piece created for television—*Sound of Soul*, written by an old mentor, Owen Dodson—that I could adapt for the stage, probably for a small royalty payment. I asked my colleague and friend Sandra Bowie to serve as associate director and sought input from Professor Dodson, my former teacher and former chair of the Howard University drama department. I figured that if I built this production at the university, the department could absorb the production costs, and the company could begin performances of the new piece while still in rehearsal for *Raisin*, the main event.

I thought I could sell this approach to the Swiss producers and the university and that it could save the international project from cancelation. I invited the production director and producing artistic director of the Stadttheater to come to the Howard campus. During that visit, I'd present *Sound of Soul*, and they'd see how it could save the project. They could decide whether its potential box office sales might cover the overages of the project.

On a colorful fall day, the *Sound of Soul* cast at Howard hosted a visit from the Swiss artistic director of the Stadttheater and the Swiss production director of *Raisin*. The Swiss delegation arrived on schedule. I learned I never had to worry about the Swiss being late for anything. The producing artistic director looked officious. He was tall, well built, and looked like someone central casting would put in a James Bond movie. He was pleasant but careful not to overplay his hand, and he definitely did not show any excitement or emotion. After all, he may have to say no. This reserved veneer made it very difficult, if not impossible, to read what he was thinking. So we were all on pins and needles. I showed the delegation to their seats in a large open room in the building where the students were waiting to perform.

The show began with an opening sequence in which Sandra, who played the mother, came into her living room and told her daughter she should stop wasting so much time playing that Black soul music and focus on the important things in her life. The daughter tried to explain how she related to this music. She said that it represented her heritage, that she wanted it in her life, and that she needed to express her emotional connection to this music. A minimal light stand brought a theatrical look to the stage. As the scene evolved, the lights changed, and the students emerged around her, close to the floor. They replicated slave ships through movement while chanting and singing an African song of slavery.

From there, the show moved into Black music of slavery times, music shared on the Southern plantation, some spirituals, and some Black religious contemporary tunes. With dance, song, plantation costumes and props, fans, and stools, the revue moved from that period to music of the twenties, thirties, and forties, and then to the doo-wop music of the fifties. In a cavalcade of performances, the students reproduced performers such as Bessie Smith, Billie Holiday, James Brown, Louis Armstrong, Duke Ellington, and Sam Cooke. Integrated into the production were moments of touching dance and instrumental interludes set to movement.

The production ended with highlighting the great Black groups of the fifties, including Gladys Knight and the Pips, The Temptations, and of course, The Supremes and many of their iconic songs, such as "Stop! In the Name of Love." I had the students dress in the costumes of each period and each singing ensemble. The effect was glorious and sounded like we were playing clips of these many legendary entertainers. When the Supremes sequence finished and the final scene moved back to the mother–daughter opening with which the production began, the Swiss director and his production director for *Raisin* jumped to their feet. They shouted, "Bravo, bravo, bravo!"

I could hardly believe my eyes. This very reserved and conservative middle-aged man began acting like a teenager, dancing in the aisle, waving, and clapping for more and more. We had no doubt we had achieved our goal. They were definitely impressed.

"The Swiss are going to love this!" he said.

Sandra and I had fashioned *Sound of Soul* into a hit. The dean even met with our European guests and impressed them with his enthusiastic support of the project. We spent hours developing a timetable and final plans. The Swiss producer and director agreed that *Sound of Soul* could more than make up for the financial deficit to support the project's expenses. Finally, all parties agreed to all the terms. The project was on, full steam ahead.

Ed and I flew to Switzerland first to prepare the host environment for the American company's arrival under Sandra Bowie's supervision. Ed was invited to join the group. He would work with the advance team at each site and handle the finances for any side tours we might book for *Sound of Soul*. Even Owen Dodson was invited to Switzerland for the opening night since he had written the original television script.

The producing artistic director of the Stadttheater offered to host Ed and me at his flat in St. Gallen. The plan was that the two of us would come to Europe before Christmas and spend the holidays with Wolfgang at his Black Forest retreat. There, we could address any unseen issues prior to the group's arrival. We would return to his St. Gallen apartment after the new year, just before the group arrived. Wolfgang provided housing, as it turned out, for the entire four-month project. This generous gesture was one of the experience's best parts, giving me a far more nuanced understanding of different cultural beliefs, customs, and ways of life.

By the time we went to Switzerland, my Ed and I had been a couple for four years. His support gave me the courage to venture out and take these risks. He agreed to quit his job and become the American business manager for the tour. We agreed to give up our apartment in DC so we could be free to stay in Europe for however long the tour might run. We put all our furniture and belongings that we couldn't take with us in storage. Then we boarded an airplane for a place I had visited only once.

My buddy George and I had played St. Gallen on that first European tour. How odd it would be to return to this same small

Swiss country town. Only this time, I would be attached to the Stadttheater. What followed were a series of high and low experiences that, at times, took my breath away and, at other times, made me feel I had failed in every way.

Ed and I arrived on schedule a few days before Christmas. At first, I had no reason to think of our host as anything but heterosexual given that there were numerous pictures of him, his wife, and his daughter all over the apartment in St. Gallen.

We were driven to our host's country retreat in the Black Forest, where we were to spend Christmas. It looked like a picture-book Swiss chalet, all wood and glass. The town was high in the Alps. Everything was covered with snow. The light of the moon beamed so brightly on the snow that I could see everything as if it were daytime. I discovered this artistic director was bisexual when he introduced Ed and me to his partner, who lived with him in their fabulous and spacious contemporary condo in St. Gallen. A photo album of their last vacation in some exotic tropical paradise had been left on the coffee table in the living room. The pictures included many nudes on the beach. The director and his lover or boyfriend, ex-wife, and child had all vacationed together as if that were normal. I was told they all loved nude sunbathing. There was no apology or hesitance in sharing these body images, some of which one might call unflattering, of normal people taking off their clothes in public.

I felt like the backward, unsophisticated American, an uptight novice behind the times. I felt like I had been protected from the real world and now was being given a chance to explore the fantastic, openly free European life beckoning me.

To my delight, our host went on to say we were going to take a sleigh ride into the forest, pick out a Christmas tree, and cut it down. As if we were in some lavish movie, the four of us—our host, his male companion, Ed, and I—found a beautiful tree well over ten feet tall. That night, the stars were all out. Everything smelled like pine incense, only stronger. The air was crisp and clean—what a beautiful, unreal moment.

We cut down this majestic tree from the Black Forest and tied it to a sleigh behind a four-wheel drive vehicle. As we got ready to drive away, with the tree in tow, our host paused and pointed to an area. He said we were very close to the Austria–Germany border. Ed and I saw the border barricade as we drove this freshly cut, gorgeous tree back to the retreat, making a trail through the snow.

We hung candles all over the tree and drank hot chocolate, lit the candles, and sang Christmas carols. Later, we walked to the town center for midnight Mass at the local church, an old, probably tenth-century, classic, simple Gothic stone structure that reminded me of the chapel in *The Sound of Music*.

The holiday made the beginning of this tour very special for Ed and me. We met an alternative family that really seemed to work and saw that a loving relationship need not be traditional to be happy. We learned that love—not roles defined by others—defines a relationship. The director and his boyfriend, ex-wife, and daughter had created a sense of family. I witnessed that the traditional family unit was not the same in everyone's lives. We stayed at the retreat in the Black Forest through Christmas and then drove back to St. Gallen in time to meet the group arriving from America.

I was responsible for fifty-five American entertainers, some students, some faculty, some professional divas, all in Europe for the first time. Because the production was an educational and professional performing experience, Sandra Bowie and I had arranged to teach classes to the students during the day, wherever we were performing or rehearsing. Performances—sometimes two, even three a day—were given in the evenings. At times, if more tickets could be sold, midnight performances would be scheduled, making it the third show in one day.

With a final count of more than one hundred performances during this four-month tour, with every performance selling out, the schedule left little time to travel beyond the confines of the tour. Somehow, we managed never to miss a social occasion. After we enjoyed the lavish after-parties, though, exploring each new place or city where we performed was beyond our stamina.

Our hosts at these events ranged from European royalty to various ministers of culture and other high-ranking government officials. The crème de la crème of society showed up at many of our evening performances: business magnates, politicians, artists, and academicians filled the seats. We were the talk of every town, and for the first time in the history of the Swiss theater, fights in the waiting lines to buy tickets became common. Most performances ended with roses being thrown on the stage at our feet. We received four months of this European star treatment. Time to eat or even sleep could barely be carved out. Such were the many demands of audiences and admirers. We seemed to live on fumes.

Most of the time, the experience was incredible, but there was always a price to pay. Management signed contracts for additional work without my consent or involvement; it seemed they wanted to get more and more from the performers. At one point, much to my surprise, someone from management was sent to collect signatures on a document. By signing, the performers agreed to extend the touring dates and make a cast recording. By the time the envoy came to me, all other signatures had been obtained.

When I asked why I was not informed first, I was told that the management didn't feel I needed to be concerned. I quickly learned this was the Swiss company's way: get what you want by any means necessary. In this case, they would first approach the less sophisticated students and hungrier professional artists for their signatures before asking me, the American associate director, who might have negotiated better terms and more protections for the performers and musicians. Nonetheless, I, too, signed the contract.

By the end of the tour, I felt as if I, and the rest of the company, had often been nothing more than paid workers who worked hard for the money, much harder than we had expected. That thought was not always pleasant.

As was predicted, *Sound of Soul* not only returned the original financial investment made by the Swiss, saving the entire project from cancelation, but also yielded an enormous profit for the Stadttheater. While rehearsing *Raisin* during the day, we performed *Sound of Soul* just about every evening. Once *Raisin* opened, we alternated performances, sometimes *Raisin* during the day for matinees and *Sound of Soul* at night or vice versa.

This tour, and any extension, required students and faculty to possess a very high learning curve and work together to overcome all unexpected obstacles. At times, the students needed to be treated as peers; at other times, the teachers needed to be mentors, and, in the most stressful times, faculty were strong parental figures providing guidance and structure for the students. Even those participants who had the least training rose to the occasion repeatedly.

For example, after surviving an avalanche that stranded our train, we were transferred to a bus. Upon arriving at the performance venue in Bern, Switzerland, we looked through the windows of our bus and saw a large red and black banner billowing in the breeze in front of the theater. It featured the pictures of three cast members in the center. Unfortunately, one of the professional actors from

New York noticed that her image was not on the banner. In its place was the face of our student, who was playing the subordinate role of her daughter.

That first night, whenever the New York actress was offstage, she complained about the banner and expressed her disgust over being replaced by a student. By intermission, she said she had become too ill to continue, and her understudy, one of my first-year students, would need to go on in her stead. Clearly, she felt the show would be canceled because of her distress.

I went to my student, who was sitting in a small corner of the dressing room with other performers. I asked the other actors to leave us alone. With great haste, they mumbled and scurried out the door. I pulled up a chair and sat very close to my first-year actress, who was young and of small stature. In a comforting way, I took her hand.

Calmly, so as not to frighten her, I explained the situation.

"Because of our train debacle, this audience waited two hours to see the show," I said, "but if you feel you can't do this, we will cancel the rest of the performance."

"I am the officially designated understudy," the student said. "I have thoroughly studied the part and am completely prepared to go on. If you need me to do this, Dr. Newman, I can. But do you think the audience will accept me as a mature mother? I'm much younger than what the character calls for."

"I realize you're just about half the age of the professional actress you're replacing," I said, "but your acting skills can make up for that difference. It's time to rely on your training. The critical thing is for *you* to believe you are the character. If you do, the audience will."

I reminded her of a professional actress on Broadway I had heard about. She, too, had been the understudy for the lead. When the star got sick and could not perform, the understudy was asked at the last minute to replace her. She was prepared and ready.

"The understudy went onstage, and a star was born," I told the student. "She was more than successful. She was brilliant and brought a new dimension to the role that the audience just loved. This is *your* moment to show what *you* can do. You have tremendous talent. That's why you are the understudy. Now is your one chance to show how talented you really are." She paused a few seconds and then turned to me.

"I can do this, and I am ready," she said.

"That's all I need to hear," I replied. "I trust you and what you've learned. I believe in your talent, and your technique will get you through. Don't try to be the actor. Be the character as you see her. Make it your role, your character, and this will work."

Actually, the professional actress had given her understudy a gift. The character's emotional catharsis (the time in the play when a character's strongest emotional persona is revealed) was in the second half. I went onstage, in front of the curtain, made the announcement of the change due to illness, and left the stage. The curtain went up. I was very nervous for my student but thought her performance would be a true test of our training program. She was brilliant! She had seized her moment. In seconds, it seemed, the audience accepted her as the believable character. She showed great confidence, grace, style, and outstanding technique. In short, she delivered a stunningly brilliant performance.

When the show was over, my student received more accolades than she could have ever imagined. We, as faculty, were prouder of our students than we ever thought we could be, and the audience thought we had brought in another professional actor to save the day. They showered our student with roses, thrown onto the stage at her feet. In that cold and snowy evening, she was the star of the show who brought warmth to that theater and audience.

The situation confirmed my burgeoning belief that the best learning takes place outside the four-wall classroom tradition. I consciously put this little thought in my arsenal of techniques that worked: students will meet whatever challenge you put in front of them if they believe in themselves and are adequately prepared.

After the *Raisin* tour ended in Switzerland, the company was individually hired to do a limited run in Paris. Most students agreed to this extension. Between the end of the Swiss production and the limited run in Paris, Ed, Sandy, and I created a small extension tour for *Sound of Soul* in Switzerland involving just the students. We hoped these performances would raise a little more money for them before they went to Paris. Because we had no advance assistance from the press, extending *Sound of Soul* on its own reaped only marginal financial success.

By the time the extended tour of *Sound of Soul* had ended, we had earned only enough money to give marginal funding to each member of the company in addition to their airline tickets for their flight back to DC. We had arranged for the seniors to graduate while on tour, so there was no need for them to return to the States immediately. The university required all faculty, including myself, to catch the return flight, as scheduled, and return to campus. We ascertained who was returning with us and who was staying in Europe and said our goodbyes.

Only two farewells in my life have brought tears to my eyes. The first was when I said goodbye to my first graduating class at Wabash College. When we shook hands, I knew I probably would never see them again. The only other time was when I watched the very last performance, forever, of the *Sound of Soul* in Switzerland. I had put my entire being into this experience. I had lived with the students and faculty. We had become one close-knit family, bonded by our circumstances, strengthened by our experiences. We all vowed to stay in touch—and some of us did.

Artistically and personally, this tour extended and expanded everyone's abilities. Many students were discovered in Europe and never returned to campus. So many stayed; there were many empty seats on our return flight. Sandy, Ed, and I knew that for all the trip's ups and downs, thrills and disappointments, we had given these students and faculty—and ourselves—an experience that molded professional careers and created lifelong friendships.

To this day, one or two students are still working and living in Europe. For others, including me, returning home was a letdown. Before long, I was back on the Howard University campus. I assumed my regular role, still full-time faculty, still needing to grow emotionally, intellectually, and professionally. I resolved to keep my mind and heart open to more new experiences that would inevitably come my way, as my European tour had taught me.

Soon after joining the drama faculty, I began a doctoral program in the School of Communications. I felt my formal education needed greater depth, and I required a better understanding of the communication process in the arts. I thought increased perceptions might help me infuse my teaching with more refined performance techniques. In short, I needed to grow even more. Howard helped: because I continued to teach full-time in the drama department, the university waived my tuition.

This doctoral program introduced me to highly respected scholars who exposed me to new thoughts, ideas, and information. This knowledge, backed by evidence from published and accomplished scholars, could transform me into an educational leader unafraid to stand up for what I believed was right. I began to understand how as a program administrator, professor, or director, I could use the communication tools I was being taught to build new arts education paradigms. I still strongly felt the best training programs would combine classroom study and live settings that forced students to reach for the stars. Finally, I decided on my goal as an arts administrator—applying my understanding of the communication process and ideal educational settings to produce the most optimal conditions for creative learning.

My father and I at my graduation from Howard University, where I received my PhD in communication theory in 1978.

My doctoral studies in communication theory also piqued my interest in exploring aspects of nonverbal communication. To that end, one of my doctoral advisors sent me to meet a renowned astrologer who lived in Maryland. My purpose was to learn about his process so I could write a paper regarding paranormal communication and make a presentation in class. On the day of our appointment, rain pelted the streets of the planned urban development where the astrologer lived. The neighborhood looked like a traditional, middle-class suburban community, not at all like the places where I'd known the more bohemian artists to live.

The downpour made reading the street signs, let alone the house numbers, nearly impossible. It was a good thing I had convinced Ed to join me because I needed his help navigating. After taking several wrong turns and backing out of the wrong driveways, we found the astrologer's house. When we reached his front door, it opened ahead of us. Clearly, our astrologer had eagerly been awaiting our arrival. He had Ed, who also had made an appointment, sit and wait while he led me into another room for my reading.

Our stargazer was of average height and build. His ordered, neat, suburban home in a middle-class neighborhood reminded me of my mother's, and he seemed to belong in the environment. I felt very comfortable. Nothing alarmed me. He greeted us at the front door and had me follow him into his study, which did seem a bit strange as he had astrological symbols, pictures, and weird-looking objects all over the room. It looked like a set for a magician's stage. He sat behind an ornate desk, picked up some papers he had prepared, and began to speak.

Ed and I had provided him with basic biographical information before the meeting, so he had previously compiled our natal charts. We were there to listen to him read our charts. He allowed us both to tape the sessions.

The astrologer began by saying that he had never seen a chart like mine and would, with my permission, like to use it as a teaching device for his astrological students. Of course, I gave my permission and was flattered by the offer. He went on to say that in most people's charts, there are crosses that represent conflicts in one's life.

"Your chart has none," he said. This meant, in his interpretation, that I had resolved my issues through previous lives and that this life would be my last time on earth because I am a very, very old soul.

"Most people will not understand your being able to see both sides of a situation or issue," he said. "They would see this capability as being insincere or duplicitous. However, it is just the opposite."

His insight rang true. I often struggled with feeling insincere. I had been called "not truthful" as I discussed both sides of an argument. And sometimes, I did feel like an old soul.

"I see you always avoiding and escaping from some dark force that stalks you," he continued. "This force will never harm you but will always hover over you. You need to be aware of it and avoid this looming threat, but do not fear it in any way."

I interpreted this statement as a reference to AIDS because the disease was prevalent during this time. Fear always seemed to be a part of our lives as gay young men. Wherever you went in the gay community and the straight community, the conversation often had an AIDS reference: who had just died, who had gotten sick, and which families had been disrupted by the disease. No one knew what caused AIDS or how it was so easily contracted in the gay community. Given the times, I found this suggestion of a looming threat not at all surprising.

The astrologer also shared insights about my likes, dislikes, fears, anxieties, and needs, all right on the mark. I had just begun the new doctoral program in communication, an area of study driven by scientific research—a long way from where I was currently teaching in the drama department. The scientists in the communication department thought of me as an artist who did not belong in their quantitative environment. I often felt like an outcast, even an alien, trying to fit in where I didn't belong. Somehow, the astrologer tapped into all my feelings of academic discomfort, my fears of failure, and my anxiety over not being able to measure up. Many of the comments he shared resonated with me as truth. *Wow, this is pretty amazing*, I thought.

"I admire you for being this special kind of person living his last life on this earth," he said. "You are a rare breed."

After my reading, I waited in his living room while Ed followed him into his study. Ed was also very impressed with his reading. One of the most significant parts of Ed's reading dealt with geography. One day, the astrologer said, Ed would end up living in California and be happiest on the West Coast.

"Don't be afraid of that draw to the West Coast," he told Ed.

After the reading, much to my surprise, Ed said he had always wanted to live in California and had been accepted to Berkeley; however, his parents had said that if he went to school on the West Coast, he could only return home after graduation. This threat had actually stopped his migration to the sunny paradise where we now live. Instead, he went to Notre Dame, continuing the fight against the snow and cold that had so distressed him while growing up in Syracuse, New York. Ed took the astrologer's prediction as welcoming words.

As I sat waiting for Ed's reading to conclude, I looked out the window and noticed all the thunderstorms had subsided. The sun was emerging. By the time we said our goodbyes and left, the weather had completely changed to beautiful blue skies without a trace of rain or wind. After hearing words that could guide us through some of life's challenges, it felt as if we had been through the storms and emerged on the other side.

In the days to come, I would often recall the astrologer's observations about my ability to empathize with both sides of a situation. I used them to help myself find solutions for conflicts with others. His words inspired me to take a hard look at my life and what was really important to me: how I could better create an environment of self-analysis from a positive base or foundation. I became more open to nontraditional approaches, such as meditation, spiritualization, and new-age thought, all different points of view and approaches to understanding life and self-fulfillment. I believed that if I could bring these different points of view to my teaching, I could better understand what motivated my students to aspire to greatness. Thus, I could become a catalyst for change and personal growth in the classroom and become an even better teacher.

As the years played out, this astrological teacher's observations and predictions proved to be true and helpful for each of us. The reading would not be the end of my experiences with the spiritual or supernatural. It was the beginning of my appreciation of how life can offer unexpected ways to reflect on the meaning of human fortunes and misfortunes.

I was hired to direct *The Drunkard*, a melodrama, for George Washington University (GW). Originally produced in 1844, the play was one of America's most successful before *Uncle Tom's Cabin*. Initially, the position appeared to be an adjunct job in which I could gain additional experience working as a director with the primarily white and international student body at GW—a sharp contrast to Howard's predominantly Black student body.

I decided to use live piano music to underscore the dialogue, just like the early silent movies always had a pianist playing music to signal the different emotions enacted in the scenes. I wanted to capture that old melodramatic feeling and style for a contemporary audience. This meant I had to find a pianist who could play the silent movie honky-tonk piano and help me develop a score. Boy, did I feel lucky when a tall, slender, good-looking young man showed up during auditions. Bahram, an international student from Iran, said he was taking a graduate class at the university and had some time he could devote to the production. Bahram was not interested in acting, but he loved the music of the period and was proficient in playing that style.

When I pressed him for more detailed specifics about his homeland and why he was studying in the United States, he became rather vague. Of course, I didn't care at the time because he fit the bill for what I needed. He agreed to help me develop a score for the show and play that score for all the performances.

As rehearsals for the production progressed, I spent a considerable amount of time learning more about this mysterious individual. He appeared very shy, extremely cautious, and incredibly guarded about sharing personal information. The closer we became, though, the more his story was unveiled. He eventually shared that he was the only son of the head of the Anglican Church in Iran. The recently deposed shah had fled the country in exile. So, too, had the head of the Anglican Church as the political situation in Iran had become extremely volatile.

For his safety, Bahram said, his father had sent him to America to stay with the bishop at the Washington National Cathedral for protection. His sister had been sent to another country, which he would not disclose, and his parents had gone to England and remained in hiding.

The story sounded far-fetched, and as I listened to Bahram

share these details, I harbored doubts about their authenticity. After all, I was in theater, and stories like these were the makings of good cocktail conversation and entertainment. I never took his stories of peril very seriously. I concluded that he was just a bit dramatic and had created the makings of a wonderful scenario that was not at all real. Yet he was such a charming, bright young man who possessed enormous talents in music and theater, so at times, I found myself getting caught up in his story and just accepting what he was saying. He always did seem a bit paranoid, though. He always looked over his shoulder as if he was trying to recognize someone or something.

Bahram talked about how nervous he was when he found himself at his lodging, which was an old stone Gothic building. He said he couldn't sleep at night because he heard strange noises and thought the building was haunted. So Ed and I invited him to stay in our guest room if he thought that would help. He quickly jumped at the invitation, and before we knew it, we had a houseguest. The arrangement was not unusual. We had hosted international students before, and by that time, we had come to really trust this young man.

The production opened to great success and ran for its allotted two weeks. By that time, we both had adopted our houseguest as a new member of our extended family, as he seemed to have no one in this country with whom he wanted to spend any time. In fact, Ed and I contrived a job he could do to pay us back for his room and board: we wanted him to supervise our housekeeper and ensure that she was doing her job to the best of her ability. This position did not last long, however, for our new housekeeping manager explained one day that he just could not tell someone so much older than himself what to do. Still, Bahram stayed on as our houseguest.

Then came the time when he said his father had summoned

him to London for a meeting with his parents—a family reunion of sorts. Bahram said the visit would be short, and he would return to the United States shortly. We assumed that meant he would return and rejoin our little surrogate family in a week or two. By then, he had become a close friend, and we looked forward to hearing about how his parents and sister were doing. He arranged a flight, and off he went.

A week went by. We did not hear from him. Then it was another week, and then another, without hearing anything. We started to worry as more time passed, but we had no address or connection in London to contact. So we just waited. Eventually, we concluded that he had decided not to return to the States and had made other plans. We were a bit upset that he had not tried to contact or message us about when or whether he would return.

Some months later, I was sitting in a barbershop, waiting to get my hair cut, and picked up a magazine. As I flipped through the pages looking for something interesting to read, I came upon an article about Bishop Tafti, the exiled leader of the Iranian Anglican Church, who had been attacked in London. He and his wife had been seriously wounded, and his daughter had escaped, but his son, Bahram, had been assassinated by Iranian government agents. He was twenty-five.

My heart sank. I had to leave the barbershop immediately and find my way home on shaky legs. It took us some time to realize that we had lost a close friend and how lucky we were to have known him. I felt so very guilty for never taking him seriously when he tried to explain his precarious situation.

Our relationship with Bahram reinforced something that the astrologer had said about taking the time to treasure each moment given to us. We must accept people for who they really are and realize that life is often much more complex than we think. "Time is fleeting and, in the larger scheme of things, very short," the astrologer had said, "so take nothing and no one for granted. Tomorrow, it may all change."

I vowed to fully appreciate every minute and every person whose path crossed mine. I would live my life to the fullest and appreciate those who shared moments of happiness and love with me. Even though these moments may be short in actual time, they can be very long and lasting in their impact on my life and the lives of others. I wished I had taken Bahram more seriously and had fully appreciated the fear he lived with each day. Perhaps I could have eased his way better somehow.

I used this philosophy at Howard when I met many African American performance icons. Because of my father's connections at the university and my becoming chair of the drama department, I was asked to host or escort these performers while they were on campus for major ceremonial visits. The astrologer had mentioned this development, too: I would be given opportunities to meet and learn from iconic legends in the entertainment industry. I followed my philosophy, drinking in every moment I had with these special people to learn what I could, good and bad, from my association with them.

I had the honor of escorting Pearl Bailey, Sammy Davis Jr., Phylicia Rashad, and Ruby Dee, to name a few. In most cases, I was scheduled for private time with the artists and their families to get to know them better and establish a trusting relationship with them. What a wonderful experience that was for me! I acquired a comfort level when dealing with celebrities and their unique needs and egos. I also had opportunities to work with some of these individuals later in my life. For example, years later, the widow of Sammy Davis Jr.

asked me to write and direct a musical revue celebrating his life for Resorts International in Atlantic City. She remembered me from the Howard host–escort program.

While working with these highly skilled, emotionally committed artists and scholars, I learned that they observe and work to understand the world in which they live. They incorporate that understanding into their art so that it touches and moves their audiences in profound ways. As I absorbed this approach, I discovered that my frailties and strengths were often reflected in my workplace. When I brought a happy and positive attitude to my work environment, others would follow with the same positive attitude. However, when I came to the workplace fearful, troubled, angry, or confused, my workplace environment took on these same qualities.

Around this time, I was given another lesson about staying present to perform life's tasks, even the small ones. I always treasured my annual appearance as Santa Claus at the DC Department of Recreation's children's holiday production. It was the climactic event of the show. I descended from the heavens in my padded red suit and flowing beard to hand out candy and toys. One day, after the Christmas spectacular had ended, I met a faculty member and his little girl walking through the hall just outside my office. At the time, he was chair of the art department of the College of Fine Arts. They stopped in front of me, and the father turned to his daughter, who had been one of the children in the Christmas show.

"Do you know who this is?" he asked. She nodded solemnly.

"Santa."

I had communicated enough of the saintly character to this little one that she recognized me without the bright red suit and the flowing white beard. I was filled with the same sense of wonderment I had experienced with Bahram's loss and the celebrities' presence: life is incredibly precious. You never really know what impact you have on others. In this little girl's mind, I was the real Santa Claus, and it was our special secret.

Over time, my fears about being under my father's shadow at Howard turned out to be totally misguided and downright wrong. He introduced me to his many friends in the upper administration, who provided occasional support when I worked on my dissertation. He provided my department with projects we created and performed to celebrate the many accomplishments of retiring employees, not to mention the additional money that came with these events for faculty and students who participated. He never hesitated to give me guidance or support whenever I needed it. At times, he did the same for my friends on the faculty and staff. His advice, support, and love were ever present each and every day.

Another gift I received at Howard was the rich and equally rewarding off-campus experiences. Just as I did at Wabash, I used my nonteaching time at Howard to explore community connections that brought enriching professional opportunities. Besides finishing my doctoral program and sharing that exciting moment with my very proud parents, I also explored pursuing one of my goals for coming to this mecca of Black culture: learning more about the rich African American heritage, community, and history. I got involved with the DC Black Repertory Company in the heart of Washington, DC, one of the most important theater ensembles in the country and an offshoot of the Negro Ensemble Company in New York City. It became yet another blessing. I was, as the astrologer had said, "born under a lucky star."

Emerging (1975–1987)

I was hired to be a production director for the DC Black Repertory Company, founded by Vantile Whitfield, a well-known arts administrator, and Robert Hooks, an award-winning actor, director, and cofounder of the original Negro Ensemble Company in New York City. These were two gifted, nationally recognized African American artists. Working with them and this talented company was simply a joy. In addition, it provided me with yet another opportunity to grow artistically and professionally.

One of my greatest professional high points was working as cocreator and director with this ensemble on *Day Break Dreams*, an original production of poetry by Gwendolyn Brooks and Langston Hughes set to music. This show was a magical artistic endeavor that found me working with some of the most creative African American actors, singers, dancers, writers, musicians, set designers, and lighting designers in the country, if not the world. These creative geniuses challenged me to be the very best I could possibly be.

The settings, or scenarios, were first created by me. I came up with various environments or situations common to most people where the action for each scene would take place. Vantile selected poetry that expressed what was happening in each situation. Then, Bernice Reagon, a MacArthur Fellowship recipient and creative genius, wrote music expressing each scenario's emotional conflict, joy, or fear. In addition to this specially composed music, we used popular music of the day to fill in the transitions, moving from one locale to the next.

We sat together as a team at one large table in the audience section of the theater. I would say, for example, "This is a moment when an extended family all comes home from work. They're living together in one small room. They are tired, beaten, and frustrated by all the conflict they faced that day. They meet and share their individual and collective stories."

In front of Vantile, on the table, were hundreds of poems and writings from Gwendolyn Brooks and Langston Hughes. He would sift through his enormous knowledge of their works and suggest one or more poems that captured the feelings of these characters. Then, he assigned these words to the actors on stage. Bernice would walk to the stage and sing the vocal passages from the poems that she wanted the actors to sing or hum. Then, she would return to the table and, like a conductor with an orchestra in front of her, direct the voices to begin as she heard them in her head. I would stage or block the scene (i.e., select the physical movements of the performers) as I imagined them happening, and just like that, the scene would come to life.

This process was spontaneous and built around the talents and skills of the actors and actresses. The moods were captivating and viscerally moving. For the audience, each moment was real and entrancing. Because we were always working as an ensemble, the performers contributed their interpretations. What resulted from working this way was simply electrifying. The words of these great poets took on profound yet easily accessible meanings. The spontaneous music Bernice created for these wonderful words took them to even greater levels of understanding and heartfelt heights. The project turned out to be one of the most dazzling theatrical experiences of my life.

The production first opened at the Colony Theatre, a restored old movie house turned into a legitimate stage theater. After a limited run there, the show was dubbed "street theater" and presented, free of charge, in the national park areas of Washington, DC. People came from every part of the metropolitan area to see it. *Day Break Dreams* also garnered acclaimed reviews and notices from critics. It was extremely successful for the DC Black Repertory Company as its traveling performances were funded through grants and donations. The production was one of the most successful of the company's season.

The repertory company became my training ground for understanding and experiencing firsthand the enormous impact of live theater in the urban community. I learned how to work with high-strung, exceptionally skilled, sometimes-demanding young artists and discovered new ways to make the themed scenarios come alive. Each time a scenario was performed in a different location, for a different audience, it spoke the same message in different ways. Some audiences danced to the music while it was happening. Often, the performances garnered a call-and-response moment, as in the Black church. Some audience members would talk back to the actors, feeling free to express their feelings with, "Go on with yourself," "Speak the truth," and "I know exactly what you mean." Each performance was different—unexpected yet exciting.

While working on *Day Break Dreams*, I became close to one of the most outstandingly talented performing artists. Lynn Whitfield went on to win an Emmy for her stunning portrayal of Josephine Baker in *The Josephine Baker Story*, but at that time, she was in the DC Black Repertory production and one of my advanced acting students at Howard.

She introduced me to her father, Valerian Smith, a popular dentist from Baton Rouge, Louisiana, who had graduated from Fisk University, a historically Black school. As a student, Lynn's father had composed music for the famous Fisk Jubilee Singers, known for their extraordinary musical skills. To this day, they are regarded as one of the best singing ensembles ever to come out of a university environment. They became the forerunners for many professional contemporary vocal ensembles, such as Take 6. After he completed graduate school in dentistry, Valerian Smith continued composing music in his local community of Baton Rouge.

One day, I was, once again, in my office at Howard University when I answered the telephone. I recognized Lynn's father's voice. He said he had a project he was hoping he could persuade me to do for him.

"It's a new musical I've been working on," he explained. "I've raised a little bit of money for production and have secured the Baton Rouge Little Theatre if only you would come down and direct it. We will accommodate your schedule and time."

I was intrigued and discussed the offer with Ed. Then off I went to Baton Rouge to explore this possibility. As it turned out, the show, titled *Supper*, was a beautifully written musical about the second line, a Southern processional parade performed by the family and guests after a funeral. It often uses umbrellas. People rhythmically move or dance in a line behind a small band as they all follow the casket to be buried. Members of the Southern Black Church community also often create a second line during Mardi Gras celebrations. The title references the friends and family who come together after the funeral. This gathering, with much food and drink, is a virtual party to celebrate the life of the deceased.

When I arrived in Baton Rouge, I discovered that all the performers were gifted amateur singers handpicked by Valerian, who often served as their dentist and vocal coach! They all shared a tight bond and worked together much like a family, which made building the production much easier. They also understood each other well and shared stories about each other.

In Louisiana, I learned how to work with communities of various people with multiple levels of performance mastery. Successfully dealing with people became one of my best assets and strengths in education and the arts. I thoroughly enjoyed hearing different types of people express their thoughts and feelings onstage and offstage. My time with Valerian's cast reinforced my belief that diversity of all kinds is a strength, not a weakness. When multiple points of view converged in this workplace, the emerging solutions addressed every problem at hand with fairness and equanimity. I found that the more I incorporated multiple points of view in my perspective, the more likely I would satisfy all the stakeholders' goals and grow as an individual.

This little show, though primarily performed by amateurs, featured two professionals heading the cast. One was my good friend Sandra Bowie; the other was Kashka, a skilled professional actor with an amazing voice. Their talents helped raise performance standards to the highest levels of entertainment. In so doing, they also provided superb examples of performance techniques for the amateur actors. The production was so successful in Baton Rouge that Valerian got additional money to move it to New Orleans, where it opened at the newly renovated Orpheum Theater in the downtown sector. *Supper* was such a hit there that it next moved to Los Angeles for a limited run.

Howard Hesseman, Sandra Bowie, me, and Lynn Whitfield at the opening night of *Supper* in Los Angeles. It was a star-studded event.

I gained a greater knowledge of how theater can help build community spirit and express a society's hopes and fears. I also saw firsthand how audiences can see themselves—their struggles, dreams, and possibilities—through the arts.

Around that time, I got another important call from the Wabash College dean, the guy who had kicked me out of the nest several years earlier and told me I had mountains to climb. This time, he was telling me the college had just established a new Owen Duston Distinguished Professorship, adding that Wabash would be honored if I'd come back for one year as the first professor to receive this honor. I was the one honored, impressed, and moved. They had not forgotten me. Each semester, I would teach two classes and direct one show.

As usual, I talked over the invitation with Ed, who agreed the opportunity was wonderful even though we'd be apart for one academic year. I agreed to accept the position and took leave from Howard to spend the next academic year back in Crawfordsville, where I stayed with John Fischer, a very good friend still on the faculty.

I missed home so much that I poured my time into my work. I could usually be found either in the theater or in my office. I spent significant time meeting and talking with the new people who had arrived since my original time at Wabash or with one or more old-timers, the senior faculty who were now running things. Because I still had friends on campus, I felt at home and welcomed from my first day, and I didn't feel isolated as a person of color.

Before I started in this new role, I made an important decision: I would not hide that I was a gay man with a partner, and I would offer no apology for my lifestyle. I thought this approach might have some consequences but was not prepared for what happened.

The first production I decided to direct and produce was *Fortune and Men's Eyes*, a powerful and dramatic story written by John Herbert about a young man's experience in prison. The play explores the themes of homosexuality and sexual slavery. I produced it in the black box area of the theater, a dark and cold space in the basement. The walls, floor, and ceiling were made of solid concrete.

I had arranged to have several rehearsals in a local prison so the students, all from families and communities with scant experience with prison, would feel what it was like to be locked up. This choice worked perfectly as the cast responded as expected to these conditions—with extreme fear, heightened frustrations, great anxiety, and anger.

When the audience members entered the theater and were escorted to their seats, the cast mingled on the set. The play was performed in a thrust performance space, meaning the audience sat on three sides of the stage. That meant most audience members sat very close to the stage. The actors were in their faces.

Once everyone was seated, the play began. Everything went as expected until the moment in the show when the bully inmate, the one who really runs what happens in the cell, grabbed his weaker, effeminate cellmate, pushed him to the floor, and began to rape him. The audience gasped with shock. I knew then that the play had achieved its dramatic impact. As the bully begins to accost this young man, all the other characters stand by and watch him have his way. The stage lights darken. The first act ends.

The second act was more of a recovery from what the audience had just seen and the characters had just witnessed. This type of play at an all men's college had an emotional effect on the entire campus.

Fortune and Men's Eyes spawned numerous discussions about the brutality of rape, the concept of man's control over man, the nature of bullying, and many other issues.

The campus was buzzing about homosexuality, something the school had never been ready to bring into the open. I had many discussions with the cast and those working on the production about these issues. I spent much time talking to my students about what it was like for me, a gay Black man, living openly in a loving relationship. Our interactions prompted self-reflection on the part of some male students dealing with their own sexual identities.

At one point, I was called into the dean's office.

"They've decided the young man who is your stage manager is being removed from your class," he said.

"Why?" I asked.

"He went to the college psychologist and shared his concerns about his own sexuality, brought to light as a result of listening to you."

They, whoever "they" were, had decided it would be best to remove the student from my class to ease his frustrations. Boy, was that a shock.

The young man in question was a quiet, sensitive person. I had never noticed him being uptight about his gayness. In fact, I did not even know or suspect he was gay. A few days later, this young man came to see me and apologized for any discomfort or problems he may have caused me. He said that the college personnel had overreacted to his concerns and that he was just fine. I told him not to worry and that I was always open to listening should he ever want to talk.

I felt that my choice to be open and honest with my students was causing a problem for the administration, and I suspected they would be happy when I finally left. Perhaps they had not expected this of their distinguished professor. Nonetheless, I was what I was.

Another issue that became a problem was my salary. To get me to accept the professorship, Wabash had to match what I was making at Howard University, which turned out to be considerably more than that made by other faculty, even those who had been there since my first experience at the college seventeen years earlier. I felt strange vibes coming from these faculty every time they saw or interacted with me. I felt uncomfortable. At times, it seemed that some were even hostile toward me.

The Black students, by and large, were welcoming and friendly. I did feel a bit of hesitation on their part about getting close to me when it became known on campus that I was gay. On the flip side, however, one of my closest friends today is one of the Black students I met, taught, and befriended at that time.

Another unique story during this period centered on the second show I directed during my last semester as the distinguished professor at Wabash—*Runaways*, by Elizabeth Swados. This collection of stories, based on the life experiences of runaway children, was set to music. It, too, was a special experience for the Wabash community. I cast students and children from the local community to play the various roles. The set was a virtual jungle gym of scaffolding, adorned with traffic signs, each giving a negative message: *Stop, No Crossing, Watch for Children, Railroad Crossing, Halt, Move Over*.

The emotionally provocative production showcased various monologues that told the stories of children who'd been abused, displaced, forgotten, or neglected. This was a world where the characters often felt alone, unimportant, even isolated from society.

One evening, as I was leaving rehearsal, I walked out into the rather ample lobby space and noticed one of my students, a senior, sitting in the corner. He looked weak, frail, and in great distress. Normally, he was an outgoing, confident, attractive, tall bodybuilder—your typical alpha male. In fact, he was one of the stars of the college football team. This young man was taking one of my classes and was scheduled to work backstage for *Runaways* in partial fulfillment of one of his practical play production assignments. I went over to him and sat down beside him.

"Is everything all right? What's wrong? You look troubled."

He said he was an identical twin, and his brother was going to another school in the state, but they regularly stayed in touch. He went on to say that he and his brother had such a close connection that they often felt what the other was experiencing; from his feelings at that moment, he knew his brother was facing a significant problem.

"Something is terribly wrong," he said. "I don't know what it is, but I know it has something to do with my brother." This knowing frightened him so much that he hesitated to call his brother. He did not want to hear whatever it was because he didn't know if he could handle it.

"I tried calling him," he said, "but I could not get through." I reassured him that it was better to know sooner than later.

"Whatever the issue," I said, "you need to act immediately so no time is wasted in helping to resolve whatever the problem is. Go back to your room where you can have some privacy and call your parents. I will walk you back to your dorm room if you need me to."

"No," he said. "It's just a short way. I can do it." I walked with him to the lobby door and watched him make his way inside.

The next morning, I saw one of his friends and asked how the young man was doing.

"What happened?" I asked.

"He left campus for home late last night," the friend said. "His brother was in a terrible car accident and is not expected to live."

I almost broke into tears myself as I realized the young man's senses had been right. At that very moment, his brother was dying, and he knew it; he felt it. Prior to that incident, I had put very little stock in a human connection so close that one person could really experience the feelings of another in real time. But this young man taught me that lesson. I now think *all* our relationships are as meaningful as those with the people we cherish. Whether we like it or not, we are connected to each other.

Sometime later, I heard that this vibrant, healthy, athletic young man suddenly had died as he never recovered from the loss of his twin. It was just too hard a burden for him to carry.

As for my future, I realized I did not want to go back to Howard. I had been a professor there for thirteen years, had gotten a doctorate, and was ready for a more challenging assignment than my previous role. If I was to remain in the education field, I needed a bigger role. I had already been the head of a department, so I considered an administrative position with more responsibility. The level above a departmental chair is that of a dean of a school or college who oversees multiple departments. In such a role, I would still have direct contact with students, which is what I loved the most, but also be able to set a vision for multiple arts divisions. I could also share my greater understanding and vision with faculty and staff as well as students. In that way, I would have an even larger impact on the academic enterprise.

So I searched *The Chronicle of Higher Education*, where these types of jobs are advertised. I applied for deanship positions at about eight institutions. Within no time, I got a positive response from most of the schools I had applied to. One was from Montclair State College, which wanted to interview me immediately. I thought this post could be stimulating, because the school is situated on a beautiful 250-acre campus overlooking Manhattan. It had just been given $5.7 million to bridge the gap between the professional arts world and academia. The new dean there would oversee all of my own disciplines: speech and theater, broadcasting, dance, music, and fine arts.

After researching the town online, I envisioned a picturesque community hidden in the shadows of New York City yet somewhat isolated by the Hudson River crossing. Swift transportation existed between this idyllic environment, known for its big homes, manicured lawns, and well-paved streets, and the Big Apple. It seemed that Montclair State was a prime location for developing programs in both the educational and professional worlds.

I felt that this could be the right move. All the fiscal conditions were right. The faculty seemed strong on paper. The students seemed to be ready for change. What could I lose by going to the interview? *I just might like it*, I thought, and, as my father would say, "The greater the risk, the greater the return."

Of course, I talked about the opportunity with Ed, who thought it was an interesting idea. If invited, I told him I would go for an interview. In no time, I was flying from Wabash to Montclair, New Jersey, first stopping in DC to talk to Ed about what the position would mean for us considering that we owned a home in Silver Spring, Maryland. We agreed that before we started making plans and discussing the various issues that could arise, I should first see whether I liked the position, the school, the faculty, the administration, and the students and see whether they wanted me.

I flew to New Jersey and was picked up at the airport by a very friendly, talkative, and informative driver from the university. The position was that of a dean reporting directly to the provost (second only to the president of the university), so my interviews would be conducted over two consecutive days. I would meet with a wide selection of university stakeholders: a search committee, faculty from the school I would head, students from the same school, some members from the off-campus Montclair community, the provost (or vice president) for academic affairs, and, finally, the university president.

All these meetings went like clockwork. Each day was filled with meeting after meeting. Even lunch and dinner were meetings in which I was expected to eat and answer questions at the same time. I was exhausted. I repeatedly thought that the interview seemed much harder than the job itself because I had no time for personal reflection or satisfying any personal needs. If I needed to go to the bathroom, it had to be between meetings.

Somehow, I got through it all rather painlessly because I had worked for years in the theater, a world where the show came first, well before satisfying any individual wishes. And since I had been trained well as an actor, talking to one audience after the next after the next was no problem.

I felt I'd made a good impression because each successive group I met with got friendlier and friendlier, as if they had talked to each other and word of mouth had preceded my arrival. Also, it was clear that the school's goal aligned with mine: its strategic objective was to build diversity in the student body, faculty, and staff. Coming from Howard at the time of the Civil Rights Movement, I felt I held a deep-seated capability for and commitment to achieving that goal.

The dean of the School of Education, the head of the search committee, escorted me back to the waiting car that would drive me to the airport to return home.

"What do you think?" he asked. "Would you really take this job if we offered it to you?"

"I could see myself working here," I replied. "I will need to discuss it with my partner, but I think it could work for me." He beamed.

After talking over the position with Ed, we realized this decision would profoundly affect our lives. We would have to uproot our comfortable, stable lives in the DC area, sell our beautiful home in Silver Spring, and reestablish a home in Montclair. We would both have to start all over again—meeting friends, developing new support systems, opening new bank accounts, learning our way around the area, and finding favorite restaurants. Despite these challenges, we agreed the change could be a great opportunity for us both. We would be just outside Manhattan, and nobody we knew who had moved to the greater New York area from Washington had ever returned.

Ed would need to transfer his career, but he had always wanted to work in New York City. We decided to accept the job if it was offered to me. Within one week, I got the call, and, as we hoped, Montclair offered me the job. I accepted the offer. We were off to Montclair.

In 1988, moving to Montclair State College (which would become Montclair State University several years later) came with challenges, issues, problems, questions, and pitfalls that I would only learn once I had been seated in the role of dean. In fact, before my position began, Ed and I drove up to Montclair in order to scout housing and open a bank account. I had just gotten my income tax return, and we had a considerable amount in my savings, so I also brought a certified check of several thousand to deposit. My intent was to select a bank, and there were two on each corner of the downtown area. I wanted to open a savings account and get checking account privileges. We went into the first bank. Immediately, a bank official came rushing over.

"Can I help you?" he said. "Yes," I replied, "I'm here to open an account. I have a certified check and a tax return government check to deposit."

He then shocked me with what came out of his mouth.

"We will first have to do a credit check on you before we can open any account."

I was stunned. "A credit check?" I said. "But I have what is like cash: a cashier's check."

He said, "That does not matter. We will still have to do a credit check first."

I could not have been more surprised. *They won't even take my money*, I thought. *What have I gotten myself into?* I left that bank in shock and went across the street to the other bank. *Perhaps this is New Jersey policy.* The next bank could not have been more different. They welcomed me, took my money, and opened a savings and checking account in nothing flat. I had just experienced, as I surmised, the, at best, snobbery and, at worst, racism I might have to deal with in coming to this position. I wondered whether this might just be a foreshadowing of what was ahead.

The college was not far from the town center of Upper Montclair. Yes, Montclair was divided into both Montclair and Upper Montclair, with two separate postal numbers. As I was told by some locals later, originally, there were very wealthy people who built huge homes and mansions on the hillside in Upper Montclair so they could take advantage of the spectacular New York skyline, which was easily seen from that location. They did not want their mail to go through the hands of the working class, who serviced them daily, because it might expose some unwanted personal information, so they applied for and received a new post office zip code for Upper Montclair. This was just folklore, but my initial experience seemed to reinforce this belief.

It was a Saturday, so Ed and I had lunch, which was very pleasant, with no issues, and drove back to Silver Spring, where we currently lived. We decided that we would make a return trip to look for housing at a later date.

My thoughts about what I could expect when I first arrived on the campus became of great concern. Would this be the attitude I would face with the faculty, students, and staff? We would just have to wait and see. I would have to take one day at a time. I'd need to pick my battles carefully and not overthink the situation, raising unneeded fear or anxiety in me. I believed I needed to stay positive regardless of what I might face.

The reactions of some faculty, staff, and a few students made it very clear to me that not everyone wanted me as their dean. Some faculty were just out-and-out hostile, made no bones about telling me their racist views, and took issue with the fact that I was gay, Black, or both. Some faculty even told me that they didn't think I was qualified for the job and that I was hired only because of my race. Others, however, welcomed me and appeared genuinely pleased that I had taken the job. This was simply the reality of what I'd gotten myself into. I needed to focus on how I could become an effective professor, administrator, and, I hoped, their leader.

Though the state had given the university several million dollars earmarked for the arts, much of the money had been designated for specific programs, so it could not be used to improve the general operational conditions. Early on, I decided I would try to find a way. The facilities had been neglected for years; many repairs were needed immediately to correct eroding conditions.

I also would need to lobby the upper administration for money for new facilities. Theater, dance, and speech were all clustered into one department. This unit also included a small but potentially popular academic program for broadcasting or television. Music was a single unit, and a fine arts department housed everything in visual arts: painting, sculpture, ceramics, art education, drawing, printmaking, and photography. A lot of work needed to be done to improve these programs' marketability and build student enrollment, which was the stated goal.

My first event as dean was a reception held in one of the hallways just outside the main theater, Memorial Auditorium. And that is exactly what it was: a large, almost cavernous high school–like auditorium. I had just left my second tour at Wabash College, where I had worked with a small student body and gorgeous facilities. Now, I faced a much larger challenge, with far more students and far worse conditions that, in some cases, rivaled those I'd found at Howard.

As I arrived in front of the building, I was greeted by the interim dean, the woman I was to replace. She had parked her car in front of the big double glass doors. As soon as she saw me, she recognized me from the interview. She immediately asked whether I would help her carry in food for this reception. Trying to be helpful, I agreed. I levered from her car a big sheet cake decorated with the words "Welcome" across the top. Not realizing she wasn't going to hold the door open for me, I turned and smashed into the glass panel of the door. The cake came toppling down all over me, the word "Welcome" covering my new suit, pants, and shoes. Talk about an entrance! It was as embarrassing as could be, but I had arrived, and everyone knew it. Trying to recover from the scene I'd just made, I thought, *I can only go up from here.* Fortunately, things did get better in some ways.

This period of my personal and professional growth as an administrator, teacher, and colleague was filled with unexpected opportunities and difficulties on a regular basis. For example, I had to give up the tenure I had earned as a professor at Howard University and earn it all over again at Montclair. All deanship appointments carry dual roles, one as dean, another as a faculty member. As such, each dean is also assigned to a particular unit or department as a professor. I was assigned to speech and theater. I had to trust that I could, again, go through the hoops of satisfying the expectations and requirements of the students, faculty, and administration. Each had a say as to whether I'd acquire tenure at Montclair. True, I was reappointed each year as dean, which also required extensive evaluations, but if I was not successful in earning tenure as a professor after five years, I would be forced to leave the university, regardless of how positively I was assessed as a dean.

Further, for my yearly appointment as dean, served at the pleasure of the university president, I would also have to be successfully evaluated by faculty, students, and upper administration. Reappointment was not automatic or guaranteed. What a risk. I constantly asked myself whether it was worth starting over at a place where no one knew me, where not everyone wanted to know me, and where I was the first Black dean. In fact, I was only the second Black administrator to run a program of this size in the whole state. The last Black administrator of an arts program had held his position at Rutgers University at least twenty years prior to my appointment, and that was Paul Robeson, a famous Black performer who had a historic name and background but not my academic qualifications. Clearly, this job was not going to be easy.

My predecessor, the previous dean, had been given a negative recommendation from his music department faculty before the president asked him to leave. The Department of Speech and Theatre would initiate my yearly evaluation and forward their review to the vice president for academic affairs, who would make a recommendation and forward it to the president for a final decision, up or down.

By that time, though, I believed in myself and my capabilities. I thought that if I was successful in doing my job—shaping the academic units that offered the best training to the students, hiring the best faculty available, and finding and hiring a talented staff who would work with me—there was no limit to what I could achieve, and tenure, as well as my yearly reappointment as dean, would naturally flow from my success.

One of my first orders of business was to actively engage the faculty to learn more about them and earn their trust so I would be considered one of their own. I had this great idea: I would make time to have lunch with different faculty members from my assigned department daily, as time permitted. We had serious as well as pleasurable, even hilarious, conversations at each lunch session. The informality of lunch provided convenient cover for difficult talks as well as a chance to share my ideas about how we could improve our school and their role in helping to make change happen.

After I started these informal sessions, the faculty began treating me as a colleague. They told me stories about their lives off campus—their struggles, their hopes, their dreams—and I shared mine. As this approach gained traction, I took it one step further.

One afternoon at lunch, I met one of the senior faculty from speech and theater. As we ate lunch, we talked about how theater was a ritual that could be seen today in the most unusual places, such as professional wrestling. She agreed. I suggested that we and another faculty member of her choosing meet in New York City and go to Madison Square Garden to see a professional wrestling match put on by the World Wrestling Federation.

"It could be a hoot," I said, and I suggested conversation and drinks at a bar of her choice after the match. She took a moment.

"Are you kidding?" she asked. "That sounds like fun."

"I mean it," I said. "It would be a great way for us to bond and have some fun."

One Friday night, we met at Madison Square Garden. I had purchased the tickets. Our seats were far enough back from the ring so that the sweat of the performers, or wrestlers, would not hit us but close enough that we could still be consumed by the crowd and excitement of the magnificent theater production taking place. As expected, it was indeed a ritual and a hoot. Afterward, we went to a typical New York City local bar, where we laughed and talked for hours about this most unusual yet entertaining outing. My plan worked. I gained a friend that night, a friend who opened the door to other faculty who also became my friends in the workplace.

I followed that experience with many nights out with other faculty at concerts, dance recitals, and theater performances in the city. These outings became a regular occurrence—the dean and his faculty having a night on the town in the Big Apple.

Meanwhile, when I used the public restrooms I had to share with the students and faculty, I saw negative, offensive, and derogatory graffiti regarding people of color and gay people, along with racial slurs too ugly to even finish reading. I could not help but hope and pray I had not made the biggest mistake of my life. An enormous headwind of negativity and hate faced me before I even started the position. If I had any hope of being successful in my job, I had to find a way to change these opinions, stereotypes, and negative perceptions.

My task seemed enormously difficult. Since I was determined to live openly as a gay man in a happy gay relationship, make no apologies for my color or lifestyle, and yet be as honest, friendly, and compassionate to others as I could be, I put aside the fear of the daunting hurdles ahead, held my head up, and prepared for the new challenges I was about to face each day. My feelings of doubt faded as I built closer relationships with my faculty colleagues. I started using these relationships as my defense against all the negativity I would encounter.

One source of negativity was the chair of one of my largest departments and my assigned home as a professor, the Department of Speech and Theatre, who had been the only in-house finalist for the position I'd just been granted. At first, he did not hesitate to show me his displeasure with my appointment. As it turned out, however, my goal of maintaining positivity against any and all odds paid off. I was able to win his confidence, and we became friends. In fact, several times when he had problems at home with his water not functioning properly, he came to our house and used our bathroom facilities to prepare for work as we had become that close.

Eventually, he even became a workplace-friendly acquaintance and one of my defenders against those who would attack me. This faculty support was critical to my achieving my goals. My recent experience as a quasi-administrator at Wabash College and my years as chair of the drama department at Howard University had shown me that the only way I could have a real impact on an entire educational arts program was to trust my ideas for making things better and selling that message to the faculty. This job as dean of the School of the Fine and Performing Arts at Montclair State College would give me the opportunity to improve the lives of the people with whom I worked.

This beautiful campus, high on a hill overlooking the New York City skyline, housed a strong regional school. However, the attitude of the faculty and students was more that of an advanced high school, as one faculty member said to me, than that of a professional training college, because that was how the institution was established in 1908—as a model high school for training teachers.

The academic units rarely, if ever, worked together across disciplines, and there were virtually no interdisciplinary courses either across or within the disciplines. For example, in painting, there was only one big art studio for everyone to use.

The fine arts department taught art as they did in high school: in one big classroom. Students were considered beginners with marginal talent, and there was no expectation that they would ever challenge the faculty. Art studio faculty and students worked together in this one large space, and all the work created by both was stored in this same space. No individual studios existed. As one faculty member said to me, "This is a place where good general arts disciplines are explored." I wanted more from this institution. I wanted to build a professional training school second to none. Eventually, I was successful in securing money from the administration to build individual art studios for graduate students, add new dance studios for dance majors, create new practice rooms for music students, and craft new performance spaces.

When I arrived, morale was so low among faculty and staff that little motivation existed for anyone to work hard. Yet these arts units had just been awarded millions of dollars for closing the gap between the academic and professional arts. Additionally, the state of New Jersey had granted them status as a Northern Center of Excellence for the Training of the Fine and Performing Arts! (Rutgers University had already received this acknowledgment for the southern part of the state.)

This was a place that needed some immediate fixes. There was a lot to do. Change needed to occur. Attitudes had to shift, too, not to mention that student enrollment was falling. I felt certain I could turn things around. I had lots of ideas and a weapon—that $5.7 million grant from the state.

What I also learned, however, was how divisive internal politics could be at an academic institution. The faculty and, at times, the students would fight over needed space, debate which program should receive additional money first, and argue about who should teach which courses. I had my work cut out for me. But deep inside me, I felt I could be up to the task. I had to believe in myself, just as I'd counseled that scared little freshman in Europe when she had to step in for a pro: "If you believe in yourself, others will believe in you, too."

Then came my first faculty meeting. It was to be the first of many regularly scheduled meetings with the faculty. They were held in the big auditorium, which the faculty also called "the main theater space." At this first all-school meeting, my heart was beating so fast that I thought I might even pass out. But I did not. Once again, my theater training and performance experiences had prepared me to be able to hide fear and exude confidence. The faculty arrived and sat in seats all over the back of the theater. I stood in the aisle, greeting each one as they arrived. They were all anxious to see what this new dean looked like and what he had to say. I was nervous as heck, wondering if they'd read my nervousness. Many had angry, annoyed, or belligerent faces because I had interrupted their plans for the day by calling for a faculty meeting.

I first asked them to sit in one place together so I would not have to yell and they could ask me any questions without having to raise their voices.

"Why not move to this center section?" I said.

They all complied. I always kept a smile on my face and exuded the charm I had learned and honed at all my previous academic positions. I wanted to demonstrate what I expected from them: positivity, respect, and joy for being there and what we had to accomplish together.

They asked me many different questions: What did I plan to do about this problem or that problem? What plans did I have for the future of the school? I had thought through this encounter and answered their questions with what I thought were winning ideas and alluded to promising futures for them all. I assured them that I would eventually address each of their concerns and make the workplace better than they could even imagine. Most importantly, I stressed that I had come to listen to their concerns and issues and then present to them, over the next year, solutions that I thought would work. Spontaneous applause erupted by the end of the meeting when those faces of doom and gloom changed into hopeful faces of gratitude and thanks for my coming to Montclair. There were even some smiles. Then, the next problem appeared.

Minority representation in both the faculty and student body was nearly nonexistent, which is to say extremely small, at best, in the larger units. I was called several unflattering names behind my back, and I was told that even many in the Black faculty and staff organization resented that I was unmarried and gay. Yes, even in the Black community, traditional family structures, in which a man married a woman and had children, were the expected lifestyle and considered normal. Anything other than that configuration was assessed as abnormal. By this time in my life, I had met or been exposed to numerous nontraditional lifestyles and unions of mixed races, cultures, and ethnicities. I had seen family groupings that had emerged or were formed as the result of great adversities or hardships. I had been shown that loving family structures were formed from, at times, financial necessity and safety needs. And sometimes, close family units had been created by individuals who simply cared for each other, who were unrelated by blood yet were drawn together, acknowledging the feelings of love for each other. Each day I came to work, I felt the tension because I dared to be different. I had landed in a very conservative environment, and I felt the need to demonstrate that there was no right or wrong way to live. I believed that as long as I showed respect for others, I could expect and would receive the same back in return. And starting with respect, we could eventually find common ground, similarities, and perhaps even love for one another. After all, in my mind, we all had to share the same space in the world.

One of my goals was to increase minority enrollment. I developed new brochures featuring smiling, happy faces of women and people of color. I spoke at recruitment gatherings and made a point to focus on potential students of color. I traveled to academic institutions that were graduating students of color and pitched Montclair as a possible academic home for them.

I traveled to international institutions, conferences, and forums to bring my message of welcome to potential diverse faculty. I spoke of our diversity initiative and desire to add more women, people of color, and international voices to augment the existing faculty and student profiles. I also asked the faculty to help identify qualified individuals who represented these diverse populations. I raised money for the recruitment of students of color.

All these efforts took time but eventually started to yield success as the profile of students, faculty, and staff began to more accurately reflect the diverse world in which we live.

Perhaps naively, I believed I could also address many of our fiscal needs, using the several million in additional dollars from the state. Was I in for a shock! Since it was government funding, the money came with enormous restrictions, guidelines, bureaucratic paperwork, and politics. Further, Montclair was a union campus. I would have to become familiar with five different contracts within which I would have to operate. If I did not adhere to them, union representatives could bring me up on charges. So I did the paperwork, studied the contracts, lobbied the union representatives, and developed strategies for identifying additional funding sources and making the needed changes.

In music, for example, millions had been awarded to a celebrity who was not directly on my faculty, had no working relationship with any of my faculty members, and, for the most part, thought very little of the existing teaching staff in the music department. Montclair was just a "pass-through" for money directed to him and his program. In no uncertain terms, he told me and the president that the only reason Montclair received the grant was because of him and his relationship with the governor. This was a problem.

This celebrity singer had just retired from a distinguished performance career at the Metropolitan Opera in New York City. Now, he wanted to discover young opera talent and groom them for a professional career. His program trained only ten to twelve students a year as opposed to the 200 to 300 current music majors. He taught his students, all older, off campus at Symphony Hall in Newark, which he felt possessed the cavernous space an opera singer needed to fill with their voice. He would listen to each potential student with this measure in mind: how their voice filled or did not fill a large concert hall.

He was a very pleasant man who thought of himself as a male diva and had an ego the size of the hall he was asking his students to fill. He identified voice teachers in New York City and Europe to coach his students. Through this program, the state of New Jersey gave him a direct appropriation of several million dollars under the name of Montclair. This type of funding, coming to the university yet not going to the academic division that desperately needed additional operational resources, created more problems than it was worth. The morale of the music faculty and students plummeted. It was easy to see why.

On the good side, I had dealt with large egos before, and my brother had groomed me in how to deal with bodacious, high-strung, uncooperative individuals. I could handle this man and this situation. I first met with my new diva quasi-faculty member shortly after I assumed my role as dean. He walked into my office as if he owned the place and I was just sharing his space. He thought he was really the one in control. I did not fight him but remained calm and cool. I did not try to control him but just listened to his point of view. And he had a point of view on everything, every subject, and every person at the university. After some time, he had spoken his piece.

"I will take everything you have said into account and develop a plan of action for how we can best work together," I said, staying calm. "I assume your desire is that we work together?" He nodded. "Do you have anything else you wish to share?"

"No, that about covers it," he said. I showed him to the door.

"Thank you for dropping by," I said. He left with a more timid posture than he had assumed when he arrived. From that day forward, he never tried to bully me again. He was always pleasant and tried charming me to win me over.

He never became a problem again, either. I felt that with enough time and the wise use of the remaining resources, such problems could be resolved, at least until I could persuade the president to unload his program—give him as little money as we could and make the program independent of the university, with the ultimate goal of severing all ties with him. That is exactly what happened.

My next task became about changing the negative conditions:

eroding morale and lack of basic unrestricted operational funds. I knew what I was doing. It was that belief in myself and my own capabilities that helped me get the students and faculty to believe in themselves and, consequently, turn around their negative attitudes.

Many times along the way, I got depressed and discouraged. Self-doubt raised its ugly head. I often had to keep reminding myself that I could do this job, achieve my goals, and experience success. At home, I spent many hours talking with Ed about my trials, tribulations, and strategies. He became my sounding board. Having a stable and loving support system at home enabled me to face the next day with optimism, hope, and positivity, which were critical for my success and that of those I'd been hired to lead. I hoped Ed would know I was always there for him, too, as he adjusted to his New Jersey and New York career dream, which had come to fruition.

For a long time at Montclair, mistrust seemed to prevail at every new junction. Some faculty still didn't like me because I was Black or gay or both, called me names, and tried to minimize my authority. But I also saw and recognized students and faculty who wanted better conditions: students who wanted to learn as much as possible but had been given no sense of self-confidence in studying their craft or themselves and faculty who were willing to commit themselves to a higher standard but had rarely, if ever, been encouraged. I felt I needed to come up with a plan that those students and faculty could buy into and believe in.

So I spent my first academic year building student, faculty, administrative, and staff respect for myself as an artist, educator, and administrator through establishing trust. I attended faculty recitals, exhibitions, student productions, and student exhibitions. After each one, I made a point to talk to the student or students involved or their teachers about what I thought was impressive, outstanding, or inspiring.

Emerging (1975–1987)

You can always find something positive to say. These appearances went a long way in establishing a positive rapport. When I could, I sent flowers from the Office of the Dean to the most important events to show our institutional gratitude. All in all, I attended more than one hundred faculty concerts and exhibitions on campus and in New York City. On occasion, I even helped fund them. I held receptions for faculty who were successful with their students and student ensembles.

The faculty of the Department of Speech and Theatre at Montclair State College (now known as Montclair State University) with me in 1988 at one of our many luncheons together.

I taught one class a term and directed one production a year for the theater program. After each show I directed with the students, I hosted a cast party where I could connect with them and they could see me in an informal setting. In sum, I worked very hard to make my presence known and my appreciation for their work evident.

Unfortunately, establishing a bond of trust between faculty and administration was harder than I had thought it would be. It took many more semesters before I saw attitudes permanently change for the better, but they did.

I thought building a team spirit would help buy time to make the many needed changes in developing academic programs and building new and improved facilities. It was clear, though, that some faculty did not want to be a part of a team or work together. After months of trying to appeal to them, I realized these particular faculty members, many of them tenured, would not come around. I looked for opportunities at other schools that they might enjoy better and slipped that information into discussions with them. I also shared news of exciting new programs at other institutions for which they were ideally suited. The choices, of course, were theirs, but I could nudge them along.

Mostly, I spent time listening to them to ascertain their personal and professional goals and how they saw themselves achieving those goals. I tried to understand their specific needs and fill them. Listening became my greatest asset for change.

Through this process, after some time, some of these faculty retired or left, and others changed their attitude. By the time I retired twenty-four years later, I had replaced more than three-fourths of the faculty on the original roster, tripled the student enrollment, and more than doubled the teaching faculty lines (the number of positions given to the College of the Arts by the central administration).

Growing into an effective, possibly even a great, leader was challenging in itself. But how to persuade others that my vision was one they wanted to embrace and work toward achieving was my most difficult goal. I needed to learn how to inspire others and create followers who would believe in me and adopt my ideas as their own while also believing in themselves. I believe that no one is born a leader; they grow into one.

As a naive and newly installed head of an entire college program, I felt that I lacked the skills and the knowledge to achieve this goal. I needed to observe where change had successfully taken place and find out how other organizations had faced and conquered this same dilemma or failed; I could learn from either.

I was determined to make my post successful. Yes, I felt I could make a substantial difference for students, faculty, and staff. But I also felt vulnerable because of my limited experience in this high-level leadership position. At the time, I was only given one secretary; one small and very depressingly adorned office from which to work; no support staff, such as an assistant or associate dean position; and no specific plans of how to improve or better the circumstances I inherited. When you take on the position of a dean responsible for multiple educational programs, the buck stops with you. I felt everyone was looking for me to come up with solutions, not negative observations: all the stakeholders, the administrators above me, the faculty and staff who worked with me, the students who depended on me to always make the right and appropriate decisions. Each constituent expected to see quick returns, winning strategies, and achievable short- and long-term goals. Yes, this was not going to be easy. However, very little in my past had been easily achieved. I only had to recall my mother's words to guide me through this challenge: "Better to cry now than be sorry later." I therefore decided to create a vision for me, the school, and each of the programs. I should take the time to listen and learn from my colleagues, my students, and my staff what they thought our collective potential was and pledge to provide whatever was needed to achieve that future—to make those goals a reality. If I believed in them as well as myself, there would be no goals too hard to achieve, no hurdles too difficult to overcome, and nothing impossible for me to make happen. I would take it one day at a time. This moment, this challenge, this seemingly impossible goal is exactly where I needed to be, where I belonged.

ACT 4

BELONGING (1988-2014)

I DISCOVERED AN organization that could help me fill in many of the gaps in my experience. It was an organization of deans who oversaw multiple arts academic divisions around the United States, Canada, and Europe. My first meeting with the International Council of Fine Arts Deans was daunting. I arrived at the participating hotel tired but excited to meet my colleagues. Not surprisingly, I was one of only a handful of people of color and women. You could count the number of Black deans on one hand. I had registered for as many sessions as were being held at this conference. But networking would also have to be my goal.

The senior deans were welcoming and eager to share their experiences. We new deans bonded quickly and spent as much time discussing our particular situations outside the formal sessions as within them. At first, I was nervous to be the new kid on the block. That feeling subsided when I realized how much I could learn from these colleagues if I put my ego aside and focused on new ideas I could use on campus.

Me around 2010 in my office after I had been successful in getting the new designation of the College of the Arts at Montclair State University.

Photographer credit: Mike Peters

I was shocked that there weren't many female deans at all. Later, one female dean told me she was asked on the elevator which dean she was married to, and she politely answered that she was the new dean. The lack of diversity I had experienced on my campus was apparently an issue for most art schools and all of academe. I also learned quickly that budget cuts and downsizing were prevalent issues on most campuses and that Montclair, with its new state grant funding, was unusual and ahead of most other institutions. In fact, I soon became the envy of my peers. The most important thing I learned was the importance of networking—sharing thoughts with others in my position who had learned much more than I had about running similar organizations.

My colleagues widely embraced me, and several years later, I became the council's secretary and treasurer for two terms. I traveled and learned of successful arts programs in many regions within the United States and in Canada, Australia, New Zealand, and all over Western and Eastern Europe. I established exchange programs of study—touring, performing, and visual arts experiences—for my students, faculty, and staff. Once again, my mother's words were reinforced: when you put in the work needed to learn, the payoff is much greater than ever expected.

Upon returning to my campus, I became aware that the entire university struggled with the problem of diversifying the profile of the students, faculty, and staff. Since I was the first Black dean ever to serve in this capacity at Montclair, I felt the weight on my shoulders to articulate and share winning strategies every time the discussion of diversity arose. That responsibility was only magnified when I went to other campuses and was forced to represent all people of color in answering one standard question: "What should we do to improve our lack of diversity?" People always seemed to look to me to give the answers and provide workable solutions. They would not hesitate to examine my faculty and student profiles for indicators or measures of success. I had to do something that worked and do it fast.

I understood that as a person of color, I was expected to know how to increase the number of minority hires on the faculty and grow the number of students of color. At times, I came to resent always being put in that position. But, like it or not, I always was expected to deliver answers. I had the feeling that many people believed that I had vast minority connections because I was part of a minority group and that I always knew where to look to fill vacancies with qualified minority candidates. "Let's get Dean Newman on the search committee," they might say. "He will ensure more minority applicants in the pool."

I often felt that I was expected to represent all minorities simply because I was one and that, somehow, I should be able to replicate myself over and over again. My frustrations grew as others' frustrations mounted. Ironically, I was seldom, if ever, asked about expanding the LGBTQ+ minority population. That part of my persona, even though I never shied away from sharing that I was part of the LGBTQ+ community, was of little interest to most people I met or with whom I would work. It was just not discussed. I guess I was expected not to mention it.

Each time a new and different-sounding or -looking individual joined the workplace, the human dynamics in our environment improved. So I believed that everyone needed to participate in achieving the change that diversity had to offer and feel an urgency in achieving that goal.

Instead, several people resented the changing face of the workplace. They felt that the change was just for the sake of change and that other conditions were being sidelined—poor facilities, eroding workplace conditions, and insufficient salary growth. It became clear that if we wanted to see significant change regarding minority hires, we needed to hire individuals who would be agents of change, regardless of their race, ethnicity, nationality, gender, or sexual orientation. My new goal was to bring these agents of change to the faculty, the staff, the student body, and all who worked in my units.

That meant ascertaining the strengths and weaknesses of each unit. I supervised and helped each unit determine its strategies for improving its workplace with regard to race, ethnicity, and gender. I then helped each design an academic action plan with realistic timetables for each goal cited in the plan. I always sought each unit's thoughts and suggestions and then contributed. I made sure they believed they were in control of their destiny and that I wasn't simply telling them what to do and how to do it. There was only one way to meet these goals: together.

One success story occurred when the theater department was looking for a new costumer for play productions and a teacher for classes in costume design and construction. An upper administration officer in the provost's office, a person of color, told me about a candidate she had advised to apply for the position. She said he was extremely creative but nontraditional, so he might slip through the cracks of the standard search committee process. She gave me his name. I investigated his application discreetly. I found him to be a talented young person of color with a progressive attitude toward theater and design. I mentioned his application to my contacts on the department's search committee, adding my strongest endorsements. They, too, became intrigued and invited him for an interview.

The interview with the dean was part of the formal process. When this young man entered my office, I knew he was special. His poise became immediately obvious, and his knowledge of costume design, as demonstrated by his portfolio pictures, was equally impressive. Before I knew it, he had won me over as someone who would bring talent and depth to the faculty. By the time the interview ended, I had learned, without his ever saying anything specific, that he was an openly gay artist from Puerto Rico with strong ties to Spain.

As a faculty member, he never failed to excite and stimulate all the students he worked with. He also designed some of the most unusual and thought-provoking costumes that we had ever seen for the musical *Sweet Charity*. I served as the director for that production. His costumes were so creative that the reviews for the production mentioned how stunning they appeared. They also wrote about the timely or contemporary approach he had taken with the female costumes, as though he was a leading fashion designer out of New York City.

Everyone was blown away by his ideas, his execution of concepts, and the magical effect they had on audiences. He was simply brilliant. I later asked him to help decorate the school hallways for the Christmas and Hanukkah holidays. He was so very out of the box in his approach. He designed and created Christmas trees that hung upside down from the ceilings, interspersed with Hanukkah symbols, lights, and ornaments. You walked through the hallways amid a sparkling sky of holiday joy that compelled you to look upward for the holidays. People talked about these designs more than they talked about their holiday plans. Artistic discussions emerged as to how he was able to achieve these designs. For instance, how could they hang from the high-ceiling hallways without falling? The question became the mystery of the day.

If I did my job adroitly, I could take all the feedback from the faculty, students, and staff in each unit and develop a school-wide plan for the College of the Arts of the future. The process might take several years to achieve, but I felt that my college and all its stakeholders were up to the task. I believed in them, and, in turn, they came to believe in me. We went to national discipline-related meetings with these goals in mind, always keeping our beautiful brochures within arm's reach. We used "diversity" as a normal, positive word in our everyday language. Slowly but surely, things changed. More diversity in the workplace, classrooms, and offices became apparent. The fear of difference evolved into acceptance and inclusion.

As the workplace attitude shifted, I was thought of as a responsive, caring leader who connected with all people: white, Black, male, female, gay, and straight, from numerous regions, countries, and ethnicities. My plan was working.

Yearly, we assessed our achievements, or lack thereof, tweaking each goal so that the faculty and students could also reassess their achievements and failures. I instilled the concept that failure is a remarkable learning tool. One only needed to get up and begin again; eventually, success would be achieved. This principle appeared to work regularly. I set high goals, and again and again, the faculty, staff, and students rose to the occasion to achieve, if not surpass, the desired ends. Every chance I got, I talked about "our plan," the vision for a new organizational structure, and a better, more diverse workplace. Anyone who happened to enter my office during this period saw large pieces of paper taped to my walls—spreadsheets on display, prompting discussions on what we were trying to achieve.

I had committed myself to building programs of distinction and to use all my resources and abilities to convince the upper administration to support this vision. The College of the Arts would not just be a cluster of programs strung together but a unit with its own goals and ideals and trained diverse and mainstream faculty, staff, and students to meet the changing dynamics in every industry and most work environments.

Our proximity to the Big Apple helped. I would often see students gazing through the windows of the rehearsal rooms at the Manhattan skyline. Each time a student saw those bright lights streaming through the windows, our goal was reinforced. The arts of Manhattan were within our reach.

As the skill levels and capabilities of the students grew, so did the enrollment. As the diversity within the ranks of faculty, staff, and students improved, so did the need for better and more facilities. I continued to lobby the upper administration for better facilities and resources and was often successful. As facilities and resources grew, so did the skill levels and capabilities of our increasingly larger number of students. We had created a circular effect of success. I could see the growth, measure it, encourage it, and shepherd it, building one element on the other. It also helped when Irvin Reid, the second Black man to become president of the college, embraced the goal of improving diversity on the faculty, staff, and student rosters, which helped my programs grow in multiculturalism. He also spearheaded the effort to achieve university status.

As the college grew, I refined my vision and strengthened my resolve. I had created a surrogate faculty family of artists who regularly challenged each other, the students, and me to be better, think more broadly, and believe that there was nothing we could not achieve if we worked together as one unit.

It was time for the next step—determining which programs had star potential. Because I did not want to fight the political battles for changing all existing programs, I focused on initiatives that could bring new dynamics to the table. I wanted to use a few programs as a drawing card for each unit. In this way, we could build enrollment and attract even more talented faculty and students who might otherwise choose to apply to more popular, better-known programs whose financial resources exceeded those of our state school.

One such program was musical theater, which became my model for introducing and building a new academic curriculum and theater facility. Not unlike jazz studies, musical theater was a less-than-popular discipline for the conservative full-time faculty I had inherited. Most faculty from all divisions spoke with disdain for such programs, claiming they drained resources needed for the basics. I would always retort with the reality that programs like musical theater bring in far more resources for basic core instruction than singular arts programs could ever generate on their own, an economic reality that benefited the entire unit.

So I had to convince the existing faculty that they needed this new program and develop a curriculum before I could even make the first hire, the individual who would champion its development and approval. My plan was first to target sympathetic faculty in theater, dance, and music to convince them to develop a curriculum that represented each of their disciplines but merged into one major, a nationally competitive musical theater program for the college. A few years later, I convinced one faculty member from each department to work collaboratively toward this task. I promised that if they were successful in getting the program approved, I would take responsibility for building new facilities to house it and securing additional resources that met the needs of the existing academic programs. Both sides energetically embraced the deal. The result was phenomenal.

By the time I retired from the university, the musical theater program had become a program with a national draw or attraction, auditioning more than 600 applicants a year for twenty new majors a year. The faculty for the program had more than tripled in size, and I had built a new $35 million, 500-seat theater in which the students could perform. These achievements inspired the faculty, students, and university administration to believe my vision could attract financial supporters and donors. It did. The university received its most significant gift to date—more than $5 million to support its investment in the arts.

During this period, I went to numerous fundraising development seminars. I learned how to set fundraising goals; how to identify, cultivate, and inspire people with my vision; and how to persuade all members of the community to embrace that vision. I learned how to attract those with resources and guide them to donate to my programs. I also learned how to lead our supporters, people who expressed an interest in the arts, to become donors who actually supported the arts with their financial and social resources. I loved the development process and realized that my theater training had paid off in major ways. I had been trained in how to raise money to support play production, but I broadened those skills and discovered abilities I never knew I possessed and had never fully used. Though the process felt oddly familiar, it was exciting.

Establishing the George Segal Gallery, an exercise in patience and tenacity, was a great fundraising success. Its story illustrates the ups and downs, the hopes and dreams of creating something extraordinary and new for an organization.

Me with a gracious donor, the then Montclair State University president, Susan Cole, and our inaugural performer, Mikhail Baryshnikov, at the opening of the Alexander Kasser Theater in 2005.

Once the university had agreed to build a new theater for the performing arts, I decided to kill two birds with one stone. Parking on campus was at a premium. Faculty, staff, students, and even administrators constantly complained about inadequate parking on the

Belonging (1988–2014)

campus. Since Montclair was primarily a commuter school, the need for additional parking grew each year as enrollment expanded. At the time, all parking was in outside lots—not a very efficient way to use valuable campus land.

Architects who wanted the university's business recommended designs for a new parking structure connected to the theater. But a parking garage does not yield the most attractive visual concepts for any university campus. Susan Cole, the first female president of the university, decided to carve out a space for a high-end restaurant in the project; it would serve as an anchor. She hoped it would draw off-campus people to spend money at the university. Also, a restaurant complements a performing arts complex relatively well.

As the project progressed, however, no restaurateur embraced the idea. The space designated for a restaurant remained large and empty. That's when I suggested we build an art gallery instead. I argued that it, too, would draw off-campus people and be an attraction unto itself. She pondered the idea and said she'd support it with one proviso: I had to find a financial donor after whom we'd name the gallery. My next challenge stared me straight in the face.

Once again, I did my research and learned that my current gallery director, who operated a very small art gallery across the hall from my offices, used to work for the George and Helen Segal Foundation, which curated the art of the famed New Jersey sculptor. In the sixties, Segal introduced *Happenings*, a program of spontaneous arts gatherings, on his large estate in southern New Jersey. It boasted green meadows and life-size sculptures that had become popular and valuable over the years. Segal had gotten his friends and family to pose for his sculptures. They would sit for hours while he completely covered them with plaster and made models of their forms. The models were then bronzed to create lasting images so realistic and extensively detailed that people who saw them would think they were real people frozen in time and space. In every way, these works were stunning.

George had died in 2000, but his daughter and widow still ran his estate and managed hundreds of his works, still housed and displayed in chicken coops and workspaces converted into gallery space. No formal gallery carrying his name existed anywhere in the state or, for that matter, the country. I also learned that his daughter had graduated from one of our arts programs. What a coup it would be if I could make a marriage between the George and Helen Segal Foundation and Montclair State University! I took my idea to the president before approaching the foundation. She liked it. However, the foundation would need to come up with a substantial donation to gain naming rights for a gallery.

I arranged a meeting with the foundation through my gallery director. The initial gathering went very well, except they made it perfectly clear that they had no cash to donate. They considered a cash donation tantamount to the foundation buying the name. That they would not do. However, the thought of establishing a gallery dedicated to George on a university campus intrigued them, particularly in a parking garage, as that would be something George himself would have enjoyed. Further, the family liked the idea of creating a place where more people would have access to George's art rather than establishing a gallery in a more exclusive downtown urban area. Segal was all about art for and of the people.

I reported what I had learned to the president. She understood but was unwilling to move from her position that a deal would only be consummated with a substantial donation. Both sides appeared to be immovable, so I came up with another plan. What if I could persuade the George and Helen Segal Foundation to donate pieces of art instead

Belonging (1988–2014)

of money, and the university could install that art at the entrance to the campus—right in front of the entrance to the George Segal Gallery, directly adjacent to the new theater? Every time audiences visited theater events, they would walk past these beautiful sculptures.

After many more sessions of negotiations with the university and the foundation to get everyone on the same page, a contract was signed by the university and the Segal Foundation: The foundation would give seven pieces of life-size sculptures, valued at more than $7 million, to the university on permanent loan. It also committed to furnishing a specially designed room for George Segal's paintings, which could be rotated with replacements each year—valued at more than hundreds of thousands of dollars. Thus, the George Segal Gallery on the Montclair State University campus was born. This project attracted many more donors to the university, dramatically increasing fundraising in addition to providing top-quality artistic memorabilia for the entire academic community.

Me at the George Segal Gallery opening with the gallery director, Teresa Rodriguez. The opening exhibition featured many pieces by Segal, some of which can be seen in the background.

BETTER TO CRY NOW

Photographer credit: Mike Peters

Associate Dean Ronald Sharps, Assistant Dean Linda Davidson, and me next to one of the contemporary pieces of art exhibited in the Segal Gallery.

I then realized I had existing programs under my supervision that could be both fundraising tools and a means to bring heightened public attention to the college. At Howard University, the students learned so much by working side by side with professionals on the European tour of *Raisin* and *Sound of Soul*. What if students could work with professionals at Montclair?

I inherited Summer Fun, a program performed on campus in a university facility, from the previous administration. For some reason, the original program had fallen into a dispute between its creator, a faculty member from the theater unit, and the university administration, which was funding it. Each side wanted to control how each dollar earned from ticket sales would be spent. The result was a legal battle, ending with the faculty member keeping the Summer Fun name but moving it off campus and the university creating its own program, TheatreFest, an Equity regional professional company supervised by the dean, that operated during the summer months.

I felt fully capable of producing and supervising this professional wing of the college since I'd started a musical theater program at Howard and understood that, to succeed, TheatreFest needed public attention. Also, I fully embraced that students learn more from working in professional settings with accomplished performers. I hired an artistic director to run the professional summer theater operation, including the day-to-day operations, and select the plays to be presented. The artistic director also would hire all the professional actors, designers, and crew for each production. I would be the executive producer, providing all the financial resources necessary.

The artistic director I selected, Phil Oesterman, was particularly up to this task as he had been successful with the off-Broadway, Broadway, and West End, London, production of *Let My People Come*. He produced and directed this award-winning and successful production and also possessed numerous professional connections in New York City. He had all that was needed to be a major force in building a successful and financially rewarding summer program for the university.

He was a pleasant man to me, but in this role as artistic director for TheatreFest, he could be, and often was, a terror, even bringing people who worked for him to tears and humiliation. But this, too, I believed, could teach students how to work in the professional business world of the theater, which, at times, was a cutthroat environment. I tried to stay out of the day-to-day operations and the artistic decision-making. I did ask, however, that he work with and employ as many students and faculty as possible. In reality, that goal seemed to always result in a small number. Only after Phil resigned several years later and I took over the artistic leadership role did the number of students and faculty increase. Phil was simply more professionally focused and had little interest in arts education.

TheatreFest was a costly endeavor, but the good it generated within the community and the university was immeasurable. People talked about the productions as if they were mounted specifically for them, which, of course, many were. However, the main goal was always to garner attention from the New York press to establish a name and reputation in the highly competitive New York metropolitan area.

One of our first success stories with TheatreFest was the production of *Bus Stop*, a romantic comedy written by William Inge. This production starred Jerry Hall, then girlfriend and companion of Mick Jagger, the English rock star. He was present for many of the final rehearsals and the production run, which, if I remember correctly, was for two consecutive weeks in Memorial Auditorium, a thousand-seat facility. It sold out because Jerry Hall was an enormous draw for the theater. As you might imagine, students and faculty alike were beside themselves just to get a look at these two notable figures. And they were not disappointed: the campus community often saw Jerry Hall sunbathing topless on the grassy area just next to the theater. It was a sight to behold. There was always a buzz about this production.

Several artists who participated in TheatreFest showed just what true professionalism was all about. One such person was the great Carol Channing. We produced her one-woman show after one of her many Broadway appearances in *Hello, Dolly!* for which she won a Tony Award, the highest and most prestigious award for performance on Broadway. She was the consummate professional—never late or ill-prepared and always in character. If you saw her onstage or offstage, she gave you Dolly with that unique voice that became her trademark.

As we prepared for her opening-night performance, I went to her dressing room to call her to the stage. I knocked on the door.

"Come in," she said. I opened the door, and to my surprise, there she sat, surrounded by intravenous poles with what appeared to be a saline solution and vitamins to help give her energy. Sitting beside her was her husband and personal physician, Harry Kullijian, who seemed to manage her every move. He smiled at me and said he would do the lighting and sound check and would be right there. I closed the door and went to the stage to wait for him.

Within minutes, he appeared and looked out at the empty seats in the audience where we had set up a place for a lighting and sound designer. He started giving directions to the lighting technicians and designers.

"Ms. Channing will be standing here," he said, "and doing—" His voice faded. Before I knew it, he had fallen to the floor and was struggling to breathe. I rushed to his side and shouted to the stage manager to call for an ambulance. My next thought was to get his wife, Carol Channing. Someone had already done that. She came rushing to the stage and took his hand.

In a few minutes, EMT professionals appeared and prepped him to be raised onto a gurney. As this was happening, he spoke to his wife.

"Please, Carol, I will be all right. You go right ahead with the show tonight. Your audience is expecting you. You cannot disappoint them."

"Yes, dear, yes, dear, yes, dear," she replied. "I will be at the hospital as soon as the performance is over. Don't worry. I will carry on."

In a few minutes, he was gone, and she was back in her dressing room. In two hours, she reappeared as the Carol Channing from

Hello, Dolly! to thunderous applause. What a professional. She was flawless in her performance that night and every other night for the entire run of the show. No audience members ever suspected that something so tragic had just happened to her.

As planned, we rushed her to the hospital. The next day, the papers revealed what had happened. She stayed an additional week after her performance schedule had concluded while her husband recovered. They flew back to California together, where they both lived. What an example for all of us about being a professional in times of crisis. The show always goes on.

Jedediah Wheeler, executive director of arts and cultural programming at Montclair; Bill T. Jones, the first artist in residence at the Kasser Theater; and me in 2008. Bill had just won a Tony Award for best choreography for the musical *Spring Awakening*.

All of us, students, faculty, and staff, learned many other lessons from this program. Other artists, such as Rita Moreno, Phylicia Rashad, Debbie Reynolds, and Tommy Tune, all legendary award-winning performers, provided stellar one-person shows, complete with backup dancers or singers and orchestras or small, powerful musical ensembles.

Each brought special qualities and shared their unique, distinguished careers, illustrating and sharing how they started, why they were in the theater, and how they had become great, successful performers. For example, Leslie Uggams, actress, singer, entertainer, and recording artist, a Manhattan legend, performed *Master Class* by Terrence McNally, the story of Maria Callas, one of the world's greatest opera singers, giving a master class to a student. She superbly recreated this character through a ninety-minute monologue. Each night, the audience gave her no less than a ten-minute standing ovation after each performance. She was such a fine and exceptionally gifted artist. The role seemed made to show off her extraordinary abilities.

Rani Jenkins, Louis Johnson, me, Lynn Whitfield, and George Faison at the premiere of *Heaven and the Homeboy* produced by TheatreFest at Montclair State University. This was a rare star-crossing moment—George Faison and Louis Johnson both choreographed *The Wiz* (George on Broadway and Louis for the movie).

Similarly, in one of the most demanding roles in any play, Ellen Burstyn was brilliant as Mrs. Carrie Watts in *The Trip to Bountiful* by Horton Foote. It seemed to me that her character had the most spoken words ever written in a play for one character. I discovered she was also an ordained minister when, between performances, she married two cast members in our garden next to the theater—another special experience for us all. George Faison created and premiered a new musical, *Heaven and the Homeboy*, as part of the TheatreFest season.

However, the highlight of my experiences with this program was when I agreed to produce and direct the hit musical *La Cage aux Folles* by Jerry Herman, the comedic story of a gay couple whose straight son is marrying a girl whose father is a very conservative politician. The couple lives over a popular gay nightclub. Numerous scenes take place in the club and feature Les Cagelles, a twelve-person ensemble of drag performers who work at La Cage. This was the first Broadway musical that broke barriers for gay representation when it became the first hit that centered on a homosexual relationship.

The show's act 1 finale, "I Am What I Am," was adopted as the "gay anthem." This became my opportunity to deal with and share gay life on the stage. The production sold out just about every performance. It featured more than 200 costumes, multiple changes within songs while the actors were singing, wonderful dance numbers, glorious lighting effects, spectacular settings for each scene, and a powerful message that never failed to bring the audience to tears each night.

I had my brother and family members come from Washington, DC, to Montclair to see this production. He was so entertained, as was my whole family. They repeatedly thanked me for giving them such an uplifting experience. Boy, was I proud. I had successfully produced and directed a gay play that everyone, even my super-straight bully brother, loved.

Me sitting on the stage with the cast of
La Cage aux Folles at Montclair State University.

The professional satisfaction was not unlike my experience producing and directing *Triplets*, a new original musical written and composed by Mark John Richard, my very good friend with three first names. It starred the remarkable Ruth Brown, the legend from the movie *Hairspray*. These were some of the hardest-working yet best times of my life.

When discretionary money became less available, I persuaded the performing arts divisions to establish a performing arts fee for all students enrolled at the university, just like the athletics surcharge all students paid. In exchange for their payment, students were given free access to all arts performances on the campus during the academic year and the summer. We ultimately expanded the summer program to run throughout the academic year. The reasoning was the same: everyone at the university benefited from these programs. The performing arts charge for all students yielded millions of additional dollars annually for the performing arts operational programs. While serving as treasurer and secretary for the International Council of Fine Arts Deans, I suggested this concept as a national model. As I understand it, it was adopted by other institutions of higher learning.

My arts programs brought so many talents to Montclair that the university established a reputation for excellence in theatrical production with the New York City press corps. We were receiving good to outstanding notices, reviews, critiques, and coverage for many programs. The publicity helped bring many other successful actors and actresses to campus. Some worked directly with students through master classes or just provided successful role models through dialogues with students in question-and-answer sessions. Celebrities worked with the students, faculty, and staff on numerous projects. Seeing students respond so positively to observing high-caliber performance techniques and getting encouragement from seasoned performers was greatly rewarding.

Me with Whoopi Goldberg at the Montclair State University graduation ceremony. Her master class for our students meant that they and I could learn from a legend.

One such celebrity who taught a master class on campus was Whoopi Goldberg, who listened to students perform monologues they'd selected, critiqued them, and returned a week later to hear their work again, modified using her feedback. To my surprise, she offered two students roles on her new television show—quite a triumph for the students and the program.

I also had the same success in the late 1990s or early 2000s, when I invited Zubin Mehta, a renowned New York Philharmonic maestro, to conduct our orchestra in open rehearsal as a type of musical master class. We added advanced instrumentalists from the community to our student orchestra. The wonder on the students' faces and delight on those of the community musicians was immeasurable. Neither would ever have gotten a chance to perform for the maestro. They all so rose to the occasion that Zubin Mehta expressed numerous accolades for their technique, levels of musical emotion, and demonstrated love of music. Whether you were watching or participating, it was inspirational.

I had learned from my days at Howard how important it was to bring top-tier professionals into the academic environment whenever possible. They never failed to inspire, motivate, and encourage the professionally bound students and enlighten others. Also, exposing faculty and staff to these professionals helped us all grow.

All my efforts relied on a team of people, students, faculty, staff, and volunteers. The more I put myself in the public eye as a leader, artist, director, and teacher, the more vulnerable I became. At times, I endured hateful or unnecessarily harsh critical reviews and, even occasionally, unflattering comments from critics who did not like me taking on so many different roles at the university. Not everyone agreed with my educational philosophy. I had to accept that my choices would sometimes generate backlash from those who had not enjoyed the opportunities I'd been given or from individuals who had nothing but negative comments to share. In short, I had to control my ego and not let negativity from others distract me from achieving my artistic or educational goals. I learned how never to become defensive and to accept that not everyone wanted me to succeed. I could endure these opposing forces because I believed I was in my position to provide opportunities for the students and faculty not to be liked.

I discovered and learned so very much from these most successful artists. I kept my feet on the ground, listened even more, accepted comments from others (even the unflattering ones), and if appropriate, used their thoughts to grow even stronger. I found my happiness within myself, not from my accomplishments. I strived to maintain humility, embrace self-reflection, and always keep my eyes looking forward. These were the commonalities I found in all successful professionals.

In 1994, under President Irvin Reid, Montclair State College had become Montclair State University. It certainly had grown into university status. By 2011, I had shaped my three units into a College of the Arts with a Department of Theatre and Dance, a Department of Art and Design, a School of Music, and a School of Communication and Media Studies, each nationally or internationally recognized. Growth was evident in other departments, too. The School of Business took on a new direction by establishing a more professional training program using business leaders from the Tri-State area, and new dormitories were built. Additionally, international programs had become a part of all the university's schools and colleges. Students were doing projects all over the world. We established the first exchange program with the famed Moscow Conservatory of Music in Russia and recorded with the New Jersey Symphony. The arts were leading the way for high-end education for the entire university. I had begun encouraging the development department to initiate dialogue with Sony to provide state-of-the-art equipment for a new broadcast facility. Montclair was on the move.

Jedediah Wheeler, Susan Cole, and me on the stage of the newly built Alexander Kasser Theater at Montclair State University.

I intensified the academic programs of study and attracted a greater number of talented students and faculty who previously would never have considered coming to Montclair. As the programs grew, so did I, professionally and personally. I developed a reputation for having built nationally competitive arts programs and made friends and colleagues all over the world. I began to feel part of something much bigger than myself. I was building a legacy, a future for hundreds and even thousands of students who discovered pride in being an artist or scholar and who would bring untold gifts to the larger community.

I may have started with only one secretary as my office support staff, but eventually, I hired an associate dean, an assistant dean, and numerous support staff who helped run the College of the Arts. Together, we built a learning center that rivaled some of the better arts schools in the nation.

But my personal life seemed to be on hold. Ed and I had really developed a strong bond as a couple. Ed had gotten a wonderful job in New York City and commuted to the city each day. In fact, we had purchased a house right in downtown Upper Montclair, and the hourly luxury bus service to Midtown, Port Authority, left from directly across the street from our little Cape Cod Craftsman townhouse built in 1911. We both worked hard but were lost when it came to New York City. We knew nothing and no one except for work colleagues who lived in Manhattan. We became known as what New Yorkers called "the bridge and tunnel crowd," commuters or Tri-State people who rarely came into the city except for an event or business.

Then we met Mark John Richard, the guy with the three first names, by chance just a year after we'd moved to Montclair. It had been a challenging year for both of us, so we decided to vacation in Puerto Rico, a popular gay-friendly getaway at the time. We booked a large room at a gay resort on the beach, facing the water, in the Condado District, within walking distance of restaurants, stores, and nightspots. We just needed to relax, have some fun, and renew our love for each other.

Belonging (1988–2014)

Ed Snyder and me in Puerto Rico after we first met Mark John Richard.

After a day at the beach, we came back to our first-floor room and saw a crowd on the terrace of the room across the entryway. They were chatting about the man staying in the room on the top floor: Mark John Richard. Apparently, he was popular in the bar and on the beach.

As I shamelessly eavesdropped, the guys also raved about a hot young man they'd tried to pick up in the bar the night before. He sounded like one hot Puerto Rican hunk! As they talked, Mark John Richard appeared on the arm of the young man they'd just been swooning over. He smiled politely at the assembled vacationers, turned, smiled at us, and continued up the stairs to his room with his newfound date.

No one said a word. Ed and I returned to our room, escaping the tension of the moment. We laughed and enjoyed the serendipitous occurrence.

The next morning, we went to the common breakfast area to get coffee and sweet rolls. To our surprise, there sat Mark John, lounging and beaming from ear to ear. He looked happy as a lark, clearly thrilled that he had been seen with the hunk. We introduced ourselves and shared what we'd seen the previous evening when he had swept in, looking like he'd just won the prize of the night. We laughed until we felt we would split in half.

From that moment on, we became best friends. By the end of the vacation, we all realized we lived close to each other. He lived in New York City while we were just across the Hudson River in New Jersey. Mark John was a youthful-looking older man about ten years older than me. We talked, drank, and smoked cigarettes, quite the fashion of the day, for hours that turned into days. Before we knew it, we were saying goodbye and making arrangements to meet back home.

Once we arrived at our respective homes, we met the very next evening for drinks in New York City. John Mark became our guide, showing us the New York opportunities that had captured his attention and filled his life with joy from the 1950s to the present day. He took us all over the city, showing us the best places to eat, the best places to drink, and the hottest places to hang out. After a few months, it became clear this was a friendship that was going to last.

He told us stories of his days as an executive producer for "a prominent advertising agency," including gossip about the celebrities he had worked and socialized with. He had mingled with numerous stars, won copious advertising awards, and created some of the most popular commercials I had grown up seeing on television.

Mark John showed us the pedestal he used to display the Jane Russell Maidenform bra in an iconic commercial of the 1950s. He had produced Dinah Shore, another historic Hollywood figure, in one of the most award-winning commercials for Holly Farms. He told us how he had traveled to Ireland to produce the Irish Spring soap commercials in which every costume was made from towels.

Mark John told us the great rigging and behind-the-scenes gimmicks he used to make commercials that looked simply natural on film. He produced a series of Jif Peanut Butter commercials and wrote the famous line, "Choosy mothers choose Jif Peanut Butter," which later became "Choosy moms choose Jif."

He told us he was the first to use an integrated cast in Procter & Gamble commercials. He told many stories of his experiences working and partying with Rock Hudson, Tab Hunter, and Anthony Perkins, all gay, so he said, all legends in the film industry. Mark John was a consummate storyteller—no doubt one of the reasons he was so good at advertising.

It wasn't unusual to go out to dinner with him, watch him engage in conversation with a stranger at the table next to us, and then listen to him make up the most outrageous story. He'd say he had traveled the world and had just met us, his friends from years ago, that very day. He was such an engaging storyteller that he often read to Ed and me, as entertainment, new writings he had created either that day or the day before, all parts of several novels he had underway.

Me with the incomparable Ruth Brown, a legend, at the opening-night reception for *Triplets*.

BETTER TO CRY NOW

Just after he retired from his prominent advertising agency, I convinced him to let me produce and direct his original musical play, *Triplets*. Advanced Montclair students arranged the music. I worked with Mark John on adjustments and rewrites, then came back to the rehearsal room and set the new changes with the actors. During these times, I observed him to be the happiest in his life. The musical revue featured the legendary Ruth Brown. The production gave him the joy of being a writer for the stage again and allowed me to feel the exuberance of working with a close friend who I came to think of as part of my family. When friends or family, as artists, combine their resources and talents, often the best work is achieved.

Mark John Richard was a unique, talented, and loving individual. He said he was the youngest of three children who immigrated to this country. His father was Italian. His mother was French. We came to accept the estrangement between him and his birth family. Rarely did he call or speak of them. In fact, when he died and the estate attorney contacted his family, they replied that they had no interest in connecting with him or his friends. His attorney told us that he requested no service or ceremony at his passing. I had to convince the attorney to have, at the very least, a celebratory event to announce his several donations to various charities. The gathering would give recipients an opportunity to acknowledge his many gifts publicly.

The ceremony was held at a private club in Manhattan in an upper room of this old turn-of-the-century building. We had been there before; it was one of his favorite places, where Mark would have us meet him for dinner. It was so very much a Mark John Richard place, with mahogany-paneled walls, original Tiffany glass ceilings, and the smell of old money, opulence, grace, and style.

At this ceremony, his attorney shared with us the fact that Mark John's personal life was very different from what he had communicated to us. He had changed his name and many particulars of his family background. In fact, the lawyer said he did not know what was true and what Mark John had made up. But it was clear that he had created his persona and lived in that persona for numerous years. He had created his history.

I began to realize that Mark John was one of our life guides as well as our friend. After he died, Ed and I felt we'd lost a close family member, a brother. After processing what the lawyer said, we decided to accept the Mark John Richard we knew, just the way he represented himself, rather than unravel the truth behind the man we knew. For, in the end, we didn't care what he made up or what was real. It had become our reality of who we thought he was. What really mattered was that he was a caring, loving individual who became our best friend, our adopted family member. He gave us his unconditional love for life, his vast understanding of the world, and his profound wisdom and respect for human behavior. He showed us the old New York City, introduced us to his friends who had been the backbone of the NYC gay community for decades, and took us places we had never discovered. Our feeling that we were outsiders, "the bridge and tunnel group" who didn't belong, no longer existed in our minds. We felt we had become part of the New York City gay community and had established long-lasting friendships and connections.

Mark John was always supportive and guided us when we needed him, like an angel. There was no doubt he was sent to be a pillar in our lives, a shoulder on which we could stand to find our own pathway. We loved him so very much, and when he died, we unabashedly and openly grieved his passing.

I wish I had listened even more closely to his pearls of wisdom, such as "always be aware of your surroundings and those with whom you share space and time." Ed and I became better people for having known and been touched by this amazing man with three first names: Mark John Richard. Now that we were better settled in the Greater Metropolitan New York City area, Ed and I reexamined our professional futures. Ed had finished his doctorate at Columbia University, landed a job at Novartis Pharmaceuticals, based in Basel, Switzerland, but with its US campus in East Hanover, New Jersey, and I had been very successful in building Montclair into one of the best regional universities in the United States, one with an outstanding national and international reputation. So I decided to focus on how much more I could accomplish at Montclair.

I felt that the longer I stayed at Montclair in this leadership role, the more I could achieve and the greater the legacy I could leave behind. To achieve this goal, I would have to engage the greater Montclair community beyond the university. So in late 1999, I invited community members to help hold fundraising parties and donate money to support the university arts programs. To that end, I established an advisory board for the School of Fine and Performing Arts (the academic unit's organizational structure before it became the College of the Arts).

I was given the name of a person who could help me identify other individuals who might be interested in an advisory board position and willing to support the university financially and for public relations purposes. This helpful, talented individual helped me establish the board and chaired it, serving as its leader for many years. After that, the university board of trustees invited her to join its constituency. Ultimately, she became one of the largest single donors in the institution's history. An alumna of Montclair, she very much cared about its future.

My first meeting with her was a bit scary for me. I didn't know what to expect. We met in my office around a conference table. She entered the room with such a smile and energy that I was immediately taken with her charm and grace. *I just have to form a relationship with her*, I thought. She was my kind of person—someone you could tell your greatest secrets to and who loved talking about the arts. What was to be a short meeting lasted an entire afternoon. By the end, we had bonded and considered each other friends.

When I first approached her about becoming involved with helping establish an advisory board, I was nervous but instantly put at ease by that warm and welcoming smile, her gracious and mild-mannered persona, her tenderness, and her overwhelming love for the arts. Her husband had been a saxophone player in college at Indiana University, one of the best music programs in the country. Her son, an accomplished pianist, had studied with some of the greatest musicians in the country, including Billy Taylor, a widely known jazz pianist and acclaimed music educator. It was an arts-loving family. I had a natural connection. She and I hit it off so well that I looked forward to the times we would spend together, enjoying each other's company, planning arts fundraisers, talking about the artists we admired, and learning from each other.

For one of the most original school fundraisers we planned, we used the empty 5,000-square-foot top floor of a high-rise building at the edge of campus. Construction had been completed except for that floor, which featured floor-to-ceiling windows around the entire space. An elevator opened directly into the area. My friend's husband was close to the bank managers of the building and knew they hadn't yet secured a tenant for this most beautiful space. So far, there were no interior finishings or wall coverings.

When she showed me the space, I immediately had an idea.

"Let me get my theater people in here," I said. "We can transform this space into something unique and special." That is exactly what we did. Her husband arranged for us to have access to a one-night fundraising event. She contacted her caterer to bring ovens and cooking materials and erect a makeshift kitchen.

The theater department created a *Fantasy Island* environment for this costume black-tie party. They used hanging flowers, candles, and exotic properties from the department's inventory. On the night of the event, when the elevator opened, people walked into rolling fog on the floor and mystical music and were greeted by hosts dressed in magical costumes from *Shangri-La*. It was as if they'd stepped into another beautiful, exciting world. The event generated buzz in the community for months. People from town who attended the fun-filled evening said they'd never seen anything like it.

The arts advisory board chair and I became an effective team. We had great fun together, raised a lot of money for the arts programs, and brought many new supporters to the school rosters.

This arts-loving couple introduced me to many of their friends and associates. They and their friends held dinners, lunches, and informal gatherings after arts events. With their help, many more community and business leaders became involved with the school as members of the advisory board and even financial supporters. They brought me into the wealthy community of Montclair. I encouraged these families to send their children to Montclair to study the arts because by that time, we had established stellar arts programs. Eventually, the word around town was to see and support the arts at Montclair.

Several years later, in 2007, when civil union was established in New Jersey for gay couples, Ed and I decided to have a marriage ceremony. This most supportive straight couple invited Ed and me to dinner at their country club to celebrate our nuptials. Our retirement plans came up in conversation. We shared with our hosts that we had purchased a beautiful condominium in Florida, but having been there many times, we were disappointed with living in that state. We found the weather overwhelming, with such high humidity that made most times when we were able to go there unbearable to be outside. Because of our schedules, particularly mine, the best time to take a vacation was during the summer months, which was the worst time to experience the heat and humidity in Florida. Further, the storms in Florida were like nothing I had ever seen. Our condo was on the water, and when a severe storm ensued, the windows facing the water would shake, almost pulsate, as if they were going to blow out completely. It was frightening to say the least.

"That's not the place for you two!" she said without hesitation. "You need to think about Palm Springs, California. Ever been there?"

"No," Ed said, "but we have heard about it."

"We have a home there," my friend's husband said. "How about, as our wedding gift to you, we give you our place to stay? You can go there whenever you are ready. You're both still working full-time, so stay as long as you can get away and see what you think about it as a retirement place."

We did just that, and, as they say, the rest is history. We ultimately sold our place in Florida, and in 2011, while I was still working at the university, we bought a home in Palm Springs.

We also met many other wonderful, supportive friends in Montclair—people who genuinely loved the arts, befriended us and supported our relationship, and helped make our lives rich and full of exciting experiences and meaningful relationships that have lasted for years. The perception of Montclair as the school on the hill, distant from the community, had changed. It had become the place for parties, plays, concerts, and special events.

My success at Montclair prompted me to develop an office for community engagement and educational outreach that brought rich auxiliary programs for precollege students. We held one such program for disabled young adults. Because they were mostly in wheelchairs, they were seldom, if ever, exposed to arts events. We invited them to see an appropriate professional theatrical event by the Pushcart Players in our main theater facility since it was accessible.

After the performance, we invited them into the adjacent art gallery space, just off the theater's lobby, and gave them drawing tools, recording devices, and other resources that allowed them to express their feelings about what they'd just seen. For many, it was the first time anyone had ever asked them to be creative. Their teachers were amazed at how much they retained and learned from seeing live theater. I got chills just watching them. They created some of the most interesting, stimulating responses imaginable. Some students painted pictures of what they saw or made drawings. One made musical sounds, mimicking what he had heard. And many wanted to move around their wheelchairs in rhythm as if they were dancing. Some teachers called it free-form movement, but others called it the students' way of expressing joy in their newfound creativity.

That creative day uplifted everybody involved, including the young adults, their teachers, as well as our students, faculty, and staff, including me. We all learned that creativity is never hampered or sidelined because of physical limitations or disabilities. Creativity should be celebrated as a part of us all.

As I continued to grow and flourish at Montclair, I contemplated that there might still be other opportunities I could pursue. I wondered if I could have an even greater impact on a larger scale if I explored a higher position within the academy. Perhaps I could create a bigger legacy as a college or university provost or even president. Three other colleague deans at Montclair had done just that. *Maybe,* I thought, *that is a path that holds opportunities for me?*

All that glitters is not gold, as I learned when I was recruited for several advanced academic leadership positions, including two college presidencies. Both were professional training arts schools with programs like those I had developed at Montclair.

The two colleges had similar characteristics but different particularities that presented different challenges. The first school said they were looking for a president who would oversee emerging programs and help raise standards to enhance their reputation. The second school wanted a president to integrate two disparate campuses, help build their programs, and manage the two campuses.

Preliminary interviews for both positions were being handled by executive search firms that asked me questions and requested that I discuss the respective positions with various individuals from the hiring institutions. From the beginning, the interviews became suspiciously troubling, but I went to both, believing I could make a positive difference at either place.

I was flown to the first school. There, a car met me at the airport, and a driver took me to my hotel, which was impressive. When I checked in, I found an itinerary had been left for me at the front desk. Only then did I discover that part of my interview process would include a public address to the faculty and community on the last day of my visit. As I had no problem with extemporaneous speaking, I welcomed this request without fear. In fact, I thought it might be a good opportunity to share my educational goals for arts schools, professional accomplishments, and what I would bring to the position.

Later, I was given a tour of the campus. During that tour, a faculty member approached me and shared his perception of the institution's diversity record. He said there was an arts middle school nearby, primarily populated by minority students, and that the university had no relationship with this school because, according to him, the school was a Black school. I had built an arts institution that respected and sought inclusion. At the very least, the thought of joining a school that didn't see diversity as a primary or even important goal was troubling and frustrating.

My next interview for this position was with selected members of the board of trustees. When I arrived for what looked to be a light formal buffet luncheon, chairs were brought into a formal living room to form a circle for discussion. As we went around the circle, each individual introduced themselves and asked me a question. I responded with what I thought to be an appropriate and sufficient answer to each question.

Then, an older, balding, rather large Caucasian man with a notably Southern accent asked me the question I will remember for as long as I live. I could not believe the words that were coming out of his mouth.

"If you are hired, would being a Black man influence your decision-making?" he asked. I took a minute to gather my wits before I responded.

Then I said, with the same intensity and deliberateness yet with the uttermost respect and revealing no hostility, "Being a Black man would influence my decision-making as much as your being a white man influences yours." There was dead silence in the room. If it had been scored with sound, there would have been a loud gasp for air. I politely sat, ate my small, trimmed cucumber sandwiches, and waited for a response. No one said a word.

"Are there any other questions?" Hearing none, I announced I was ready to move to the next scheduled meeting.

The evening before my major address, I called David Driskell, an old friend, teacher, colleague, mentor, and a world-renowned artist and recognized art scholar. I explained the situation and asked whether I should truly consider this post. He replied that I was talking about one of the five stand-alone art schools in the country and that it had never had a Black president. I would be the first.

I had a cultural and ethical dilemma. Clearly, this was an environment with deep racial issues that needed to be resolved. Should I hide my feelings about diversity and inclusion from these people to get the job? Or should I tell them what I truly think and who I am from the beginning, even though that may cause me to lose any consideration for the position? It was a long night before I gave that speech. I did not get much sleep.

When I arrived the next morning for the presentation, I was surprised to see the room filled with faculty, students, and staff. I opened my presentation by saying I was very happy to be with them and had thought long and hard about their position. I had concluded that I should share my feelings about diversity in the workplace and the academy.

I went on to speak about my personal performing arts background as well as my commitment to presenting diverse voices through the arts. I pointed to the art school adjacent to the campus.

"If I were your president," I said, "I would make sure we were all represented on the campus across the street. Embracing diversity would become our goal and strength."

The audience seemed to listen with bated breath. I saw from their faces that my words were hitting the mark, bringing delight to some—and fear to others. There were smiles, some folded arms, some confusion, and several nodding heads. When I came to the end of my speech, it was very clear that all assembled understood my message clearly. To my surprise, after a few minutes of embarrassing silence, what occurred next was thunderous applause and cheers.

After my presentation, very few questions were raised, but a lot of mumbling ensued. I felt the tension in the air. It seemed that it was time for me to go. I said my goodbyes, moved with alacrity to my waiting car and driver, and went to the airport to catch my plane back to Montclair. On the return flight, I could not help but think about these unusual circumstances and what they meant. If I didn't know better, I would conclude that they had just brought me in as a token minority applicant with no serious intention ever to offer me the job. But they'd conducted a national as well as international search, and I was one of only two finalists! The other was a rector from a British school just outside of London.

By the time I arrived home, the phone was ringing off the hook. It was the real estate agent who had shown me various available properties should I choose to take the job. He shared what he'd heard about what had happened as a result of my interview. "The board of trustees fractured," he said. "Those members in favor of offering you the job resigned." The board then decided to abolish the search completely and give the position to their current interim vice president, with whom I had interviewed. He put it this way: "The entire school is in turmoil about what to do next."

Clearly, I was never offered that position. I learned from that experience that saying what you think and feel can result in severe consequences, but how could I be anything but authentic? I strongly believe in the strength of workplace diversity and the inherent value of diverse voices. I just could not pretend to be anything other than the man I am. This position was just not the right fit.

In some ways, I was proud that I had stirred up so much controversy by raising questions the board didn't want to hear and, as such, had, in some small way, become an unwitting change agent for this institution. However, I could not ignore that I felt I had been used. Yes, one can say that I had spoken what many in the community wanted to hear, but I was saddened that this institution was not prepared for this truth. I had crossed the Rubicon and chosen, at that moment to my peril, to express my deepest-held philosophy and underlying beliefs about diversity as an educational necessity, not just a choice.

I had no regrets about what I had said to my first national audience and how I had acted. I felt sorry for a school, or any organization for that matter, that didn't recognize the value of diversity. I vowed always to speak what I believed in during any interview, regardless of the outcome.

The other school interested in interviewing me for a leadership position was an equally impressive academic enterprise. It also had many artistic disciplines I had been working with at Montclair and a few additional ones. I met the current president at a conference where we exchanged educational philosophies. He had encouraged, almost insisted, that I apply for the position from which he would soon retire.

That interview was also a two-day process. I met with all the appropriate stakeholders except, curiously enough, the board of trustees, who never arrived for our scheduled meeting. I sat in an empty room, alone for almost an hour, waiting for someone to enter. But no one ever did. I was later told that I would receive a follow-up

BETTER TO CRY NOW

phone call from the chair of the board of trustees. I acquiesced—what choice did I have?—and left the two-day interview process thinking I had done an outstanding job communicating who I am and what I bring to the table. But what was happening with the board?

Several days later, I received a phone call while on assignment at Carnegie Mellon's arts programs as a team accreditation evaluator for the Middle States Commission on Higher Education. To my surprise, it was the chair of the board of trustees of the East Coast arts institution where I had just interviewed.

"Our selection process is down to two candidates," he said, "and you're one. I feel the board could go either way on this hire, so please submit a written description of your goals for our school and how you'd achieve them should you become president."

I explained that I was currently out of town and would have difficulty responding to that request immediately.

"If you're still interested and want to continue to be considered," the chair said, "you'll have to submit these comments to me within the next twenty-four hours, or we will have to eliminate you in this process."

"I'll do my best," I said and hung up the phone. Another long difficult night was ahead.

I spent the next two hours writing a response to this rather unusual request, knowing full well that it possibly was yet another hurdle put in my path to take me out of contention. As required, I sent my written response to the chair that day, within twenty-four hours. I never heard back from him or anyone else.

I did, however, get a call about two weeks later from the executive search firm that had recruited me for the position. "The institution," they said, "decided to hire the other finalist." I felt deceived. I could not help but believe that I had somehow, once again, been used to leverage an in-house candidate as the safest and easiest choice. I was forced, one more time, to recognize the politics woven into the fabric of every institution and the position of president. It is not always about one's skills, talents, or even accomplishments. Sometimes, it's just about the political situation that overrides educational values and determines all outcomes.

Ironically, several months after the interview with this popular northeastern arts school, Ed and I were meeting a friend for dinner in New York City. I was engaged in conversation with our friend when a woman standing behind me interrupted my conversation. She said she thought she recognized me and asked if I had recently been on her campus interviewing for a position. She described the school to a tee.

"Yes," I replied, "but that was a few months ago."

She went on to describe my visit to this arts school and, more importantly, my impact as a result of those interviews. She said that the faculty, staff, and students felt I was the best choice for the position and that she had been surprised to hear I was not coming to be her president. She shared that the school community had raised such a fury over the board's hire that the school had entirely lost faith in the board's leadership.

"Congratulations," she said. "You did well, and I have no doubt another institution will snap you up. You will make an excellent president."

So I *had* been noticed. I expressed my deepest-held educational beliefs, and they were appreciated. I learned an important lesson that day: We all leave our mark. It may not happen the way we expect, but our impact can and will often be felt long after we leave a place or person. We always leave a footprint wherever we go.

After these two experiences, I questioned whether a more

advanced academic position was a realistic option for me. I did not enjoy the political gamesmanship I saw in these interviews for leadership roles. Maybe a provost's position would be different. One such position surfaced at a stand-alone arts university. An executive search firm once again recruited me. I thought I was particularly suited for this position because it, once again, oversaw the arts disciplines I currently manage. Despite my earlier disappointments and against my better judgment, off I went, thinking I would give this job search one more shot.

This prospect also was an arts-only university. My interviews with individual faculty, staff, and students went extremely well. I picked up positive vibrations from all encounters until I met with the president. When I arrived in his office for this final interview, I sensed an awkwardness in his dealings with me. As the interview went on, he grew rather defensive, disagreeable, and downright unfriendly. By the end of the interview, I felt he was looking at me as a threat and talking to me as if I would be coming to replace him. This encounter felt strange because I liked him and respected his role as president.

By the end of the interview, I felt as if I was being rushed out the door. Later, I heard from the executive search firm that the faculty, students, and staff all liked me and thought I would be an excellent fit for the position. However, they felt that I had completely turned off the current president. Maybe he thought I was much too slick to be trusted. *Huh?* Perhaps it was the tailored Armani suit that fit like a glove. Perhaps my well-dressed look was intimidating. Perhaps my speaking in standard American English gave room for pause or distress. Perhaps, once again, I was not "Black enough," or I sounded "too educated" for this urban arts school. Or it may have been my aggressiveness in asking too many questions. I did not know.

Regardless, I felt drained and confused and recognized that this was not the position or place for me.

After this series of interviews, I took stock and reassessed my priorities. Questions abounded: Was I willing to reshape who I was to obtain an academic leadership position that might appear attractive? Was I willing to compromise some of my values to reach a position of greater influence and initiate diversity policies?

By contrast, I already wielded power, influence, respect, and support at Montclair. From the beginning, Montclair explicitly expressed its commitment to diversity and its need and efforts to support such a goal. Should I reassess the difference I could continue to make at Montclair? Was I just feeling a need to start over and bring my talents and ideas to another institution? Was I really prepared to do that all again? Did I possess that much energy? It took a lot out of me physically each time I started a new job, established new far-reaching goals, and attacked new hard-to-achieve challenges.

The time came to seriously think about what made me happy. In the end, I concluded that a provost or presidency position would pull me further away from the academic core arts disciplines, the very reason I was in education. I understood the glamour associated with the title "president." I was aware it came with power and influence, but that wasn't what *I really* wanted. I relished working with students, hearing their concerns, understanding their needs and fears, and embracing their dreams as my own. I could continue to do that if I rededicated myself to staying at Montclair.

So after some long, hard discussions with Ed, colleagues, and close friends, I resolved to stay at Montclair and explore how far I could build this exciting program in the arts nationally and internationally.

To give me better tools and a broader perspective to achieve this goal, I applied for and received admission to the three-week summer executive leadership program at Harvard University, designed to promote leadership in educational management. There, I could explore my thoughts on upper administration and relevant issues in managing a complex enterprise. I believed Harvard would help me finish my education in university management, goal setting, fundraising, and understanding human behaviors in the academic environment.

I arrived one hot summer morning at an un-air-conditioned dormitory. The participants selected for the program were told at the first class meeting that the hardest thing at Harvard was getting admitted. Once you have been accepted, we were told, there is no longer competition for a place in the class; all discussions should come from our thinking rather than our need to impress the faculty. It was the first time in my life I had ever heard anyone, other than my family, say that I had succeeded in measuring up to my peers at the onset. I had nothing to prove, just learn.

From the first class, it was clear that this course, which followed the case study approach developed at Harvard Business School, would be challenging and a lot of work. Prior to our arrival, Harvard had sent hundreds of pages of reading material. Each day, we were asked to prepare case study materials for discussion. Because of the careful selection process, we were a diverse group of administrators. Lively discussions ensued: they were always rich, controversial, and representative of different and often divergent ideas. We debated issues from many different sides, unique perspectives, and varying viewpoints, coming up with solutions to resolve the problems in the academic workplace.

While participating, I often thought back to those days sitting in the newly integrated white school and being told I did not possess the potential to succeed. But there I was at Harvard University, being asked to share my thoughts. *What an irony. What would those nasty, bigoted elementary and high school teachers say if they could see me now?*

Learning that I determined my destiny has always been *the* lesson for me. Once I joined this think tank group from around the country, that little negative voice saying I might not measure up fell by the wayside. I never heard from it again. It took an achievement like being admitted to Harvard University to arrest my fears of inadequacy. That summer, I grew more as an educator, an administrator, a critical thinker, and even as a student than I could have ever imagined. My thoughts of self-doubt and fear of failure totally disappeared.

When I returned to Montclair, replete with a self-confidence that energized my every decision, I knew I was where I needed to be. I had finally come into my own. I had found my voice, and I believed I had something important to say and share with those around me. I felt I was whole.

With renewed vigor, I embraced the Montclair challenges. Years earlier, with the Howard students in Switzerland, I had become convinced that all students learn more deeply when they are engaged in the real-world professional pursuit of their art.

If these pursuits include the experience of international cultures, the growth is exponential. Over the twenty-four years of my tenure at Montclair, I also found that global education strengthened a respect for diversity on the local campus.

It was time for an international touring program at Montclair. I identified some funds that could be used as seed money and invited faculty to help me. I used a faculty assistant from the provost's office to administer the project. I called upon this office for more seed money, raised more funds out of my office to cover expenses for traveler participants, and developed operational protocols.

Tom Veenendall, Ed Snyder, me, and my special assistant, Gerry Caracciolo, on tour with *The Best of Broadway* in Switzerland.

Before we knew it, we had a plan: students would travel outside their comfort zone to a foreign country and perform their respective art. We built a musical revue, much like we did at Howard University with *Sound of Soul*. For our first international tour, the faculty and I wrote *The Best of Broadway*, a ninety-minute revue of Broadway music written to highlight each student's unique talents. The tour was designed to begin in the Netherlands and travel to Ukraine. I selected these two venues because of the stark differences between the countries and cultures. To help students acclimate to Europe, I decided we'd stop in the more familiar Netherlands first and then move on to Ukraine. Most students had never been outside the United States—or even the state of New Jersey—prior to this trip.

The scenario for the revue was this: The students, with their acting coach and musical director (played by the actual faculty members), are stuck in an airport waiting for a delayed flight. The location changed from Amsterdam, the Netherlands's airport, to Kiev (now Kyiv) International, the Ukraine airport, depending on where we were at the time. While waiting for their flight to depart, one faculty member asks the students to review the scenes they have been studying while the other pulls out a keyboard. And so the show begins.

The students perform selected Broadway songs commonly recognizable from many popular, award-winning Broadway hit shows, such as *Cats*, *Les Misérables*, and *Phantom of the Opera*. Each song is staged using costumes and properties that appear out of their luggage. The revue concludes when a faculty member comes running onto the stage, announcing, "The flight is ready for departure! Come on! We've got to get to the gate!" Everything is rapidly packed back into a big trunk and other luggage. The show ends as they all scurry to the departure gate.

The students were so excited about the prospect of performing in Europe that, even while we were still in the US airport, they broke into song. They almost caused a scene as passersby stopped to take in their enchanting voices, their bright, happy faces, and their excitement for what they were doing. It was magical, and it reminded me of past experiences.

The first stop of our tour was the Amsterdam airport, where we were driven by bus to the theater. We had arranged homestays for the students so they could mingle with the Dutch people. As the bus pulled up, its big windows revealed the various host families eagerly waiting to meet their new guests. The students looked worried, almost troubled, not knowing what to expect next. Their reaction gave me great pause. Had I pushed my neophytes too far, immersing them too fully in this new experience too soon?

Hesitantly, I waited while every student found and connected with their host family. We were to meet for rehearsal early the next morning at the performance venue.

The following morning, I stood outside the theater, concerned about how my students had handled the evening. To my surprise and delight, the students began arriving on the backs of bicycles, in tandem on scooters, or waving from cars with their new friends. In just one night, they had bonded with their local hosts. They were happy and excited about performing and had managed to share that excitement with their local host family. I felt relieved, confirmed, and fulfilled. I had made the right decision. They had found new surrogate families, new friends—people who shared their caring, loving spirits with them all.

The performances went off without a single problem. Once again, as it was at Howard, the students had risen to the occasion. They had surpassed my expectations and had demonstrated the efficacy of their Montclair arts training. They were emerging artists who could communicate through their craft. I was so very pleased with their success. I felt like a proud parent seeing their children grow up and become adults.

By the time we were packed and ready to go to the next location, the students were saying goodbye to their new families, people who used to be strangers but were no longer. With tears of joy, they wove plans to reunite in America as hosts and made vows to return someday soon. Saying goodbye involved lots of hugs and kisses.

From there, the tour traveled to Kiev (Kyiv)—an entirely different type of experience for the students. We were all in the same hotel near the performance venue—the beautifully restored Tchaikovsky Conservatory of Music. This beautiful building was the anchor facility for Freedom Square, where, just a year earlier, Ukrainians had celebrated their independence from Russia. Our opening-night performance marked the first anniversary of that celebration.[3]

Earlier that day, I had held a press conference. To my surprise, the primary question asked of me was why I had chosen musical theater as the content for this performance. Given the Ukraine situation, some people thought it seemed like a frivolous form of theater. I responded with little hesitation, first reminding the reporters that musical theater was the genre that had helped Americans get through slavery, the Great Depression, and other crises. Art has always been the message of hope and the expression of resistance and resilience. It is through art that great societies share their history, their dreams, and project their future. They looked at me with skepticism and disbelief. I invited them to see the show and judge for themselves.

The performance went on without a hitch, building toward the final scene from *Les Misérables*. The students' luggage had become the barricade as the audience was transported to a street in Paris. The students, now representing French rebels, took their stand, climbing up the barricade of luggage as the company began to sing, "Can you hear the people sing?" These powerful lyrics by Alain Boublil, Jean-Marc Natel, and Herbert Kretzmer speak of a people rising and taking control of their destiny. In this production, the company climbs higher and higher on the self-made barricade as the song builds louder and louder until it resounds with, "When tomorrow comes!"

At this very point, the music crescendos to the end of the song,

---

[3] As of this writing, that hall, and indeed Freedom Square, have been destroyed by the current war and attack by Russia. Today, we all feel very fortunate to have seen and experienced it when the country was still whole and beautiful. Looking back on it now, I remember the heightened joys, the immense happiness, and the enormous pride these people shared with us. They showed us their hopes and dreams for a better future, a country free from control and war. It hurts me deeply that these days are but mere memories of the past. My hope is that someday, these people will be once again free from Russian tyranny.

and the cast stands on the very top of the barricade. In the original play, the red revolutionary flag of France is waved from the top of the barricade. I had replaced this red flag with the new flag of Ukraine, celebrating its independence from Russia. One of the performers raised this enormous blue and yellow Ukrainian flag to the surging music. The flag was so large that it took my strongest actor to wave it. He was the only person in the company who was even capable of managing the unfurling of this gigantic piece of fabric.

There was one long second of silence in the theater, long enough that it felt like almost ten minutes before the audience realized what had just happened. Then, there was such an emotional outburst that you would have thought a bomb had just gone off, only it was the thunderous applause of the audience leaping to their feet, screaming, cheering, and yelling. They simply went wild. The performance came to a halt while we waited ten minutes for the applause to subside. The audience had certainly gotten the message. So did the press.

Even more exciting, at the end of the performance, the doors to the theater opened to reveal more than 100,000 people in the old Lenin Square, now Freedom Square, cheering the celebration of the first year of independence from Russia. The students got to experience an emerging nation celebrating its freedom from oppression and control.

When the tour concluded, the students and faculty had changed. Everyone looked to the future with newfound positive attitudes. This traveling performance program helped reverse their demoralized attitudes and set a high standard for everyone to achieve. They had also become much more sensitive to the needs of other cultures and each other. They returned to the campus as champions for the international experience as a learning tool. They became my ambassadors for diversity.

Leonid Kravchuk observing *The Best of Broadway* performance in Ukraine.

Student academic performance also improved. Months after returning to the campus, I was sought out by a parent of one of the tour participants. She said she had no idea what had happened in Europe, but her son was a different person as a result of the experience. He was much more responsible, serious, and diligent about studying his performance techniques and had deeper faith in his ability to communicate through his performing art. She thanked me for giving her son this opportunity.

This confirmed my belief in the importance of these experiences for budding artists. They grew as people and artists when challenged with real-life performance rigor. From that first tour, the students, faculty, and staff fully embraced the rigor of professional performance, discovering a clearer understanding and value for their artistic voices.

As my tenure at Montclair continued, I repeated this touring program many times. I used jazz studies students to stimulate the formation of a competitive academic jazz performance studies program.

My musical theater program finally took root and became one of the top five training programs in musical theater in the United States. An expanded dance program became connected with the modern dance studies department at the Victorian College of the Arts in Melbourne, Australia. Visual art programs and exhibitions were established in New Zealand and China.

That first success in the Netherlands and Ukraine became my ignition point. Many more programs and initiatives were spawned by the faculty on the strength of this first success. I hosted visiting faculty and artists from Slovakia, Hungary, Holland, Britain, New Zealand, Australia, and China, to name a few.

Teachers started creating touring projects and ideas for student learning outside the walls of the traditional classroom using their local, national, and worldwide connections. These projects ranged from *Across Boundaries*, a visual arts exhibition exchange with artists in China, to a theatrical performance of *The Dining Room* with a mixed cast of Chinese and American Montclair students, each speaking their language, performed in China and then on the Montclair campus. The audiences appreciated this contemporary Tom Stoppard play as if they understood every word spoken.

The second music program that had one of the greatest impacts on the students and faculty was the tour of the Madrigal Singers from the music department to Austria and Germany. Though a treasured learning experience for everyone, it helped their conductor, a traditional, classically trained professor, grow in his understanding of the value of diversity. This was a senior faculty member who, I believe, was entrenched in his department. He had been there for many years, working in difficult situations with minimal resources. It appeared to me that he had lost some of his excitement about what he was doing. I felt that this trip to Europe with his students could help him rejuvenate his dedication to his work and the college. With a bit of guidance, it did.

The conductor had taught the students a Medieval and Renaissance period repertoire, primarily in German and Old English. Prior to leaving on tour, they had performed successfully many times in German, even in front of some native German-speaking people on the Montclair campus. When I asked whether he thought American students singing in German—to German audiences in Europe—was a little risky, he retorted indignantly that his college language was German and that he spoke German fluently. His answer was emphatic.

"There will be no confusion," he said.

I went along on this tour as an observer. When we arrived at the first venue, I was surprised to hear that he gave a lengthy introduction to the concert and the performers—and in German! The audience responded to this in a strange way; they were confused as to why he didn't introduce the group in English. They squirmed in their seats. I could see from their confused and disgruntled faces that they were annoyed. They often acted distracted and disturbed.

Shortly after the performance, a member of the host's chaperone team came to me privately. She said she had a delicate subject to discuss.

"Of course," I said. "What's the problem?" She requested that I ask the faculty member introducing the group at the beginning of the concert to speak in English rather than German.

"His German is not clear," she explained, "and many people have complained that they had trouble understanding what he was trying to say." Apparently, his perceived fluency in German was mistaken.

"English might work better," she added, "since European audiences speak English as well as they speak German."

I promised to talk with him, but I realized that this would not be an easy conversation. He believed his language skills were excellent. *This can be a learning lesson*, I thought, *if I can avoid offending him.*

Before the next concert, I pulled him aside. I explained to him how it had been suggested to me that the audience would enjoy the concert experience better if he trimmed back the introduction and discussion with the audience. This change, I explained, would demonstrate his technical and artistic success in teaching the students German language skills.

"Focus instead on the uniqueness of this being an American performing group," I urged him, "and use the German language exclusively for the music. Trust the students to tell the story throughout their performance using the German language you taught them."

Reluctantly, he said he would make the change. The next audience's response dramatically differed from the tepid, puzzled response of the first night. All the performers and the conductor were buoyed by the evident enjoyment and pleasure the audience showed. The members of the host group, who had complained to me earlier, thanked me for listening and implementing the change. I gave all the credit to my faculty member for being so sensitive and responsive to local reactions and shaping the program to meet the needs of our audience. In no time, the local hosts eagerly embraced and bonded with my faculty member and praised him because they could really see how his students shined from his excellent teaching.

My mother always said that you can catch a lot more flies with honey than with vinegar. By the time the tour ended, I had seen a new faculty member emerge—a less arrogant and more inclusive, sensitive, caring individual. He, who had once been my loudest critic, aggressively and without hesitation, now shared the exuberance of his recent European success. He became my anchor and advocate in touting the need for more diverse experiential student learning experiences and faculty hires.

This broader vision spread throughout the department like wildfire and broadened everyone's vision about the importance of diversity. Programs such as jazz studies and musical theater flourished in student popularity. Even the classical faculty took them as serious academic pursuits. Ultimately, this respect and enthusiasm resulted in hiring new faculty to lead these areas but also prompted other faculty to make many new requests for diverse, interesting projects.

Television students and faculty did in-the-field projects in Italy. Dance students and faculty had a successful project with students in Australia. Visual arts students engaged in joint projects in China and New Zealand. Theater students established a performance relationship with students from the Shanghai Theatre Academy in Shanghai. I sent a faculty member to Shanghai to direct the American musical *Meet Me in St. Louis*.

My fledgling performance arts tours spawned an educational center that enabled and funded students to mix, on and off campus, with fellow arts students around the world. We had established and achieved a national and international vision for the arts at Montclair. In the end, these tours not only transformed the entire College of the Arts but also became the model for a university-wide Global Education Center. Such opportunities were formalized for all 18,000 students across all schools.

Not too many years later, the music department established a performance and study-abroad relationship with the world-famous Moscow Conservatory of Music, culminating in a formal articulation agreement whereby Montclair students could study in Moscow for a year while only paying Montclair State University tuition. Because of the strength of the dollar, room and board was included. At that time, it was the only program of its kind in the United States. We even invited the Moscow Conservatory of Music choir to come to our campus and participate in a joint concert of *Carmina Burana* with the New Jersey Symphony at the New Jersey Performing Arts Center in Newark, New Jersey. It was a remarkable experience, even for the New Jersey Symphony. They repeatedly spoke about how this new combined ensemble was so technically proficient and prepared and sang with such passion.

The Russian members of the group shared their feelings about how rarely, if ever, they'd been given the opportunity to employ such emotion in their performances. They said the Montclair choir exemplified this singing quality in a way they'd never experienced. The performance was so successful that the New Jersey Symphony Orchestra recorded it and released the recording as one of their great accomplishments in concertizing in 2008.

The process of transforming students into competent professional performers took hold and became the standard, not the exception. It was remarkable how quickly the students in a real-life situation absorbed what often had taken weeks to teach in the formal classroom. We all grew together and learned what we could achieve from these tours and each other.

These international experiences also demonstrated the universality of the arts, regardless of culture. Because of off-campus educational and cultural experiences, students knew they were part of a much bigger community than they had previously believed. Their eyes also were opened to universal needs, struggles, hopes, and dreams. This is what we all hope for as teachers—that our students live each day of their lives making and sharing their talents in the pursuit of building a better world than the one they inherited.

Belonging (1988–2014)

When I retired in 2012, my faculty, staff, friends, and supporters of the college threw me a party in the very theater I'd taken the lead in designing, building, and supervising. During the better part of one year, these individuals had helped plan and execute this impressive evening, from the ten-by-ten-foot painting of fifty squares—each painted by a different artist and assembled to look like a mural of my likeness—to musical theater students in full Broadway costumes performing the finale to *A Chorus Line*—only they were singing to me, calling me the "One." The university president presented me with an academic chair with a plaque that displayed my years of service, 1988–2012.

At my retirement celebration in 2012. The president of Montclair State University presented me with this beautiful academic chair.

Montclair State University students performed the finale of *A Chorus Line* at my retirement celebration. It meant more than I can say to be called the "One" by these talented performers.

My broadcasting students, along with their teachers, put together a testimonial video featuring clips of individuals I'd known throughout my twenty-four years at Montclair. They all said they thought of me as their leader and spoke of how I'd helped them make a significant difference in their own lives. Then came Melba Moore, Grammy- and Tony Award-winning singer and actress, singing me her newly recorded single to thank me for what I'd done to help her. I had directed her in *Anything Goes*, and we'd become friends.

Melba Moore performing her latest recording at my retirement celebration in 2012.

Me with the delightful Melba Moore after her performance at my retirement celebration reception in 2012.

These stories and testimonials moved me. I was satisfied to know I'd made a difference to so many people, including some on whom I hadn't thought I'd made an impact. One young man representing the dance students asked whether he could speak. He told his own story—how he had just returned from Desert Storm, where he'd served in the army, and received funding to pursue a degree. He explained that he'd come to school early each morning to get away from home because his family didn't like his decision to major in dance. They found it a disappointing, bad decision that they could not support.

My office was directly across the hall from the dance studio where this young man took his morning dance techniques class five days a week. So I would pass him as he sat on the floor in the hallway, stretching, waiting for the teacher and other members of his class to arrive. I saw him there repeatedly for several days, saying hello as I passed him by and proceeding into my office. One morning, I needed to learn more about this young man on the floor; he did not altogether exhibit happiness and did not look pleased. Yet he was somehow resolved. So I sat down on the floor with him and listened to what was happening in his life and what was going on in his mind.

Every day, he said, he had to overcome the external opposing forces confronting him at home. He struggled to find the will and courage to continue his path as a dance major. Dance was what he loved. Being a professional dancer in New York City was his dream. Yet he was being forced to question whether he was making the right choices.

He recounted to my retirement audience that after listening to his story of frustration, confusion, dismay, and fear, I had told him, "This is your dream, not anyone else's. Embrace it with everything you have going, regardless of what others say. If you don't do that, you might wake up one day and think about what you could have been if you'd only had the courage to beat the odds and pursue what you loved the most. You alone can make your dream a reality, but you have to believe in yourself. Trust in yourself, work as hard as you can, and that dream will become your future, your reality."

He told the assembled audience that from then on, each day he saw me, I asked, "How are you doing today?" He became more resolved to pursue his dream because at least one person believed he could do it. Someone had cared. My words, he said, became his motivation for completing the program. Happy and living life on his terms, he is living his dream in New York City.

Years later, one last story confirmed that my actions had made a difference in another person's life. I had retired from Montclair State University, and Ed and I were living in Palm Springs. Our next-door neighbor would go to the local gay bar for drinks every Friday and Saturday night. He urged us to come along many times. Finally, we agreed to go, saying we would have just one drink and then go home as we did not consider ourselves drinkers or get great enjoyment from hanging out at a bar, gay or straight. Our neighbor–friend smoked cigarettes, so we were relegated to sitting outside, faking that we liked breathing secondhand smoke. We did it to be with our friendly neighbor and his friends.

As we sat there, making conversation, I noticed a young woman staring in my direction. She would glance away from us for a few minutes but then, every ten minutes or so, focus back in our direction.

"Is it my imagination," I asked Ed, "or is that woman on the other side of the bar, on the patio, staring at us?" He looked.

"I think so," he said. "I wonder what she wants." As he finished that sentence, the woman stood and walked directly toward our table. I did not recognize her, but she recognized me.

"Dr. Newman?" she asked. "I know you don't remember me, but I was one of your students at Howard University, and, my God, did you change my life. Before I studied with you, I had no idea what I was doing, where I was going, or how I could get there. You changed all of that for me. I now work in the film industry and am doing extremely well due to what you taught me. I feel very blessed to have studied with you and am so very grateful."

Chills consumed my body. I could not believe what I was hearing. After all, I didn't even remember what I had done to be so helpful. Her sharing was just as emotionally moving for me, far greater than anything I had ever expected. At that moment, in a bar, one that I rarely went to, I had been reminded that I had made a difference in one student's life, much more than I had ever realized or known. This experience filled me with more joy and satisfaction of accomplishment than anything anyone had ever said or done. I recognized my work had indeed helped someone else find meaning in their life. This is the hope of every educator. I had achieved that goal. Ed and I left that bar that night, and the entire way home, I tried to figure out who that young woman was, what I had done or said that had such a lasting impact. After all, this was more than thirty years later. But really, in the end, those details didn't matter. What mattered was that I had helped inspire someone to find their path and take charge in overcoming their roadblocks, and they had found their success because of my efforts. I realized that all my work in education had not been in vain. Even though I had not been on television or the big screen, even though I had not become the performing star I had hoped to be, I had, nonetheless, left my mark. I had made a difference. On the car ride home that night, I was happy and joyous knowing that I had made a positive impact in the life of a student. And that teacher who in the fourth grade said I would never amount to anything was wrong. I had succeeded. I had made a difference. That's all that really matters.

EPILOGUE (2023)

You might wonder what life is like now, ten years after retirement. Let me first say that for Ed and me, adjusting to retirement has not always been easy. After many years of working, knowing that your reliance on a monthly paycheck and having regular financial resources coming in suddenly ending can be, at the very least, physiologically troubling and can garner a whole lot of fear. In the beginning, I often thought, *Can I really make it on a limited income?*

Even more problematic is that one's job can greatly identify who you are, how others define you, and even how you define yourself. In retirement, many people ask, "Don't you miss being considered successful because of what you have achieved? Don't you miss being looked up to because of your title, the amount of money that you earned, the high lifestyle you were able to live, the important people you were able to rub shoulders with, or the fact that because of your position, many people were forced to listen to you and gave the impression that what you had to say was so vital? Don't you miss the many friends you made in the workplace?" As my father used to say, those workplace friends are really just acquaintances, not really friends. I found that to be true.

But what is also true is that each day in the workplace, you live to work, and in retirement, you work at living. Ed and I wake up early each day to experience another opportunity to determine what we want to do and then do it. New friends have come into our lives who are following similar paths, who are happy to be alive and in control of their destiny. Let me share one last story.

Each year, Ed and I mark the beginning of fall in beautiful Palm Springs, California, by having morning coffee and tea, sweets, and fresh fruits with friends. This year is no exception. We've invited five couples to our classic 1950s abode near the airport to kick off the next cycle of weekly gatherings. It's one of the modernist Alexander homes for which this desert resort city is known.

We love our home's post-and-beam construction. The interlocked style of the wooden ceiling is all that separates us from the outside elements. We got Spanish tile for the roof insulation. That was some time ago. The years run into each other now. Ed and I have been together for forty-nine years. It's been just over eleven years since I retired and eight years since I started writing this book.

Each week, our group, or part of our group, meets at one of our homes for a coffee hour. Nothing special happens at our gatherings. We sit, talk, drink coffee or tea, and avoid political discussions. We are a group of older men, so of course everyone brings something different to the table, sometimes a unique perspective, sometimes affirming what someone else has shared. And because everyone in the group is past fifty, and some, like me, are well over fifty, no one is shy about speaking their mind or expressing their opinion.

Each of us has had a successful career and has retired or is close

Epilogue (2023)

to retirement. We all live very comfortably, and we're all gay. Ed and I say many times, particularly when we leave Palm Springs, that it is the only place in the world where you find gay couples who've been together for twenty, thirty, forty, and even fifty years and who are, by and large, happy. At some point, we've all overcome great hurdles in our lives and yet are content with who we've become: well-adjusted individuals who respect ourselves and each other. At social events in the desert, it's surprising to see someone who doesn't have gray hair or no hair and is not fashionably dressed down. We keep a very relaxed environment, always. No one dresses up like we used to do back on the East Coast. The standard wardrobe is simple: shorts and a T-shirt or short-sleeve casual shirt.

Our friends are all mixed-race couples. One was a government worker, who happens to be my cousin, and his white husband. Another is an Italian American whose husband is Filipino. A third used to be in the legal profession and is now married to a man he fell in love with when he was married to a woman; his current husband helped him raise his two children, now grown adults, after his wife died. Two other couples had professional careers and are in their second marriages.

Most were educated at hard-to-get-in colleges and have expertise that spans architecture, painting, nursing, interior design, and landscape architecture with a specialty in desert and exotic plants. So there are always differing opinions.

This group of couples relocated to Palm Springs from all over the United States—the Midwest, the Northwest, the Northeast, and the East Coast. They represent different temperaments, beliefs, styles, and unique pasts and histories. Each has an intriguing story to tell. As one of our members always says, each of us could write a book about his journey. I hope each of us does write their own story, as I have done. No one is shy about sharing their journey with each other or with anyone else who will listen.

We all have one thing in common: we survived an often-hostile world and built our lives on our own terms. We love getting together and sharing our thoughts, opinions, hopes, and dreams. We frequently travel together, try new experiences together, and share moments of great happiness together. When one or more of us needs support, encouragement, a new adventure, or just some inspiration in our lives, there's always someone ready to satisfy that need. Each of us is excited and hopeful about what life has in store. We are happy.

Ed and I are busy readying the coffee, the treat (a coffee cake we made for the occasion), cups and saucers, spoons and forks, napkins, and serving utensils when the doorbell rings. The first couple to arrive marches in like they own the place; they bring a delicate homemade phyllo pastry with a raspberry topping that makes you feel like you're about to eat something from a French patisserie. The host always determines what will be served, and no one is required to bring anything, so their treat is a welcome surprise. This particular friend is a baker, though, and is known for creating the most mouthwatering pastries. His husband is the gourmet cook of the group; *America's Test Kitchen* asks him to make their new recipes and give feedback on what they should keep or change.

The conversation begins at the door and continues as the couple finds comfortable seats. In no time, the remaining couples arrive. Because the weather is somewhat cooler in the morning, we start the soiree sitting outside until it gets too hot. Then, we move into our casita, which is big enough to house the entire group. We sit in a circle or another configuration so that everyone can see each other and

Epilogue (2023)

engage in sometimes two or three conversations at the same time. One of the group asks me a question.

"How is the book coming?"

"It is still being edited," I answer. "This editing process seems like it never ends. Every time I finish a passage, I rewrite the segment before, after, or both. It seems like I just can't stop myself from changing one thing or the other."

At that same time, another friend asks Ed about his tai chi exercise.

"Have you started doing your tai chi again since your heart surgery?" Ed begins to answer while I continue to go on about my writing and what's new about the book or my thoughts about working with my editor.

Simultaneously, another member of the circle turns to the couple with whom we shared a house on the coast the previous month.

"What was it like being away for a full month?" he asks. "How was the beach? Was it really as beautiful as the picture you sent?" Right then, Nicky, our cute, lovable Westie, appears. He loves being in the middle and demanding attention at every opportunity. Of course, that raises even more discussion. "How did Nicky like his time at the beach? Did he get along with Gracie?" Gracie is the dog who belongs to the other couple at the beach house. An answer comes quickly.

"They became great friends! They hung out at the beach with us every day. Primarily, they slept, but they also loved to watch the surfers and the paddle surfers."

Before you know it, multiple discussions are all happening at the same time. Around us is a panoramic view of the majestic San Jacinto Mountains. Though gorgeous any time of day, they are tinged by a beautiful orange hue at sunrise. Our group, busy chatting away, hardly pays any attention to it.

There is no table between us. We each eat or drink while holding the food, coffee, or tea on our laps or using a TV table set up behind the sofa or beside a chair. It's always like a family gathering, a get-together of loved ones who just want to touch base and reconnect.

In essence, the discussion is generally always the same. This is not a *Boys in the Band* gathering. We don't put each other down, make snarky comments, or indulge in witty repartee. There are no jokes at anyone's expense. No one bad-mouths anyone in the group. We all just enjoy talking and hearing each other's voices. Someone shares what trials they had or saw that week, what health issues they conquered or are working on overcoming. We talk about what is happening in town with people without housing or some other concern that has arisen since we gathered last or that one of us read about.

Our purpose is simply to enjoy each other's company and have fun. No conflict is engaged or encouraged. However, someone seems always to insert a story about an escapade from their youth, perhaps a sexual exploit or something of that nature. The stories are often repeats. Yet we sit and listen to them as if for the first time. We don't attempt to solve any of the world's problems. We just realize that we understand what they are and that each of us has our own opinion or approach to how they might be solved.

You could say we are a support group. We have nothing to prove to anyone anymore and are content to talk about a cruise, an art event, a book one of us has read, a film one of us has seen, or a fundraiser that might be worthwhile. We explore possible group activities: a new trip, a new adventure on someone's bucket list, a way to help people in need. Individuals chime in with support or build on thoughts. Then, we suggest a plan of action. Someone volunteers to develop a proposal, and we will put it on the agenda for the next gathering.

We all believe we should continue to provide support for others, perhaps just in a small way that betters the world we have inherited and helped to build. We are thankful we have earned an opportunity and the resources to do so. We just want to share our enjoyment of our little piece of heaven, our oasis in the desert, with each other and those who might also benefit from our efforts.

Importantly, we know we have each other's backs, so we never feel we are alone or just surviving. In every sense of the word, we enjoy the lives we have made, the environments we have created, the individuals we have become. I guess you can say we have all become a group of LeRoys and Clydes.

After about two hours, we bring our discussions to an end. We all get up and prepare to fulfill our plans for the day, taking with us a newly charged strength to face whatever is in store.

As we move to the door, we hug, meet fists in a goodbye gesture, or peck a quick kiss of goodbye.

"See you next week," one person says.

"I'll call you about that movie date we talked about," another responds.

"Don't forget to get me that number and address I asked you for," yet another adds.

The couple with whom we shared the house at the beach for a month this past summer gives the parting thoughts.

"Goodbye, Nicky," one says.

"We'll bring Gracie next time so you can play together," the other promises.

As we hug, touch, kiss, and leave each other, we are—each of us—already looking forward to the next time we meet. After so many years of grappling and struggling, trying and surviving, we now indeed share a wonderful life and the true joy of living. We are now what we choose to be. We are our own persons, the protagonists of our journey, our play. We are content. We are living the life that we have created, that we have earned. And that life is simply wonderful, full of great happiness, abundant joy, and most importantly, love.

Me, Ed Snyder, and our dog, Nicky, ready for Christmas at our home in Palm Springs, California, in 2023.

ACKNOWLEDGMENTS

IT DOES TAKE a village. The following are individuals whom I would like to thank for helping me with the *Better to Cry Now* project:

Edward Snyder
Mary Grace Snyder
Lorraine Ash and Lorraine Ash Literary Enterprises
Dawn Newman-Marti
Norita Chaney
Sandra Bowie
Richard Wesley
Ronald Sharps
David Driskell
Melba Moore
Robert Pimm
Mike Peters
Steve Hockstein and Harvard Studio Photography
Steven Katzman
Gregory Battle

Gary Morris
Chris Sutton
Kevin McKee
Gary Hermanoski
Jerry Del Monico
Drew Johnson
Damiano Locovocci
Irv and Pam Reid
Antoinette Doherty
Diana Bucco St. Lifer
Larry Londino
Patty Paroh
Diana Benson
Tom Leonardis
Whoop Inc.
Wabash College
Howard University
Montclair State University
The George Washington University
DC Black Repertory Company
Wayne State University

And all the many other individuals who helped me gain self-confidence and the belief that I had something to offer in establishing a footprint.

ABOUT THE AUTHOR

Photographer credit: Steven Katzman

GEOFFREY NEWMAN, PHD, is dean emeritus of the College of the Arts at Montclair State University in New Jersey. He was the first holder of the Owen Duston Distinguished Professorship from Wabash College in 1987 and received the prestigious Amoco Award for Theatrical Excellence from the Kennedy Center American College Theater Festival in 1979. He helped establish the Department of Theater at Wabash College in 1970 and served on the faculty of the drama department from 1975 to 1986, during which time he was appointed chairman of drama (1982–1986). He then served as the founding dean of the College of Arts at Montclair State University from 1988 to 2011. He now resides in Palm Springs, California, with Ed, his husband and soulmate of forty-seven years.

www.ingramcontent.com/pod-product-compliance
Lightning Source LLC
Chambersburg PA
CBHW060518080526
44586CB00012B/523